Using the e
2 Investiga
Part 2

A Unit for teachers

Published for the Schools Council by
Macdonald Educational, London and New York

© Schools Council Publications 1974

First impression 1974
Second impression (with amendments) 1976

ISBN 0 356 04355 X

Library of Congress Catalog Card Number 74-81802

Published by
Macdonald Educational
Holywell House
Worship Street
London EC2

850 Seventh Avenue
New York 10019

All rights reserved. No part of this publication may be reproduced, stored in a retrieval system, or transmitted, in any form or by any means, electronic, mechanical, photocopying, recording or otherwise, without prior permission of the publishers.

The author of this book is:

Margaret Collis

The members of the Science 5/13 team are:

Len Ennever	Project Director
Albert James	Deputy Project Director
Wynne Harlen	Evaluator
Sheila Parker	
Don Radford	
Roy Richards	
Mary Horn	

Typeset by Waterlow (Dunstable) Limited

Made and printed by Chorley & Pickersgill Limited, Leeds

The Science 5/13 Project

'Science 5/13' is a Project sponsored jointly by the Schools Council, the Nuffield Foundation and the Scottish Education Department, and based at the University of Bristol School of Education. It aims at helping teachers to help children between the ages of five and thirteen years to learn science through first-hand experience using a variety of methods.

The Project produces books that comprise Units dealing with subject areas in which children are likely to conduct investigations. Some of these Units are supported by books of background information. The Units are linked by objectives that the Project team hopes children will attain through their work. The aims of the Project are explained in a general guide for teachers called, *With objectives in mind,* which contains the Project's guide to Objectives for children learning science, reprinted at the back of each Unit.

Foreword

Margaret Collis has been a valued friend of the Science 5/13 Project since it began. It is entirely appropriate, therefore, that having written *Using the environment,* she should, with characteristic generosity, have made it part of the Project's materials.

For years before the Project even began she, I and others in the Project team had been working together on teachers' courses and on committees of various kinds, exploring child-centred ways of working in science and helping to introduce them into schools. Margaret Collis still works tirelessly with teachers of varied experience, and in the generous atmosphere she always creates, they respond with enthusiasm and conviction. She has become aware of their doubts and uncertainties, and having accumulated a great store of first-hand knowledge about what they really want to know, she offers them the advice they need and through it the confidence they seek.

Both knowledge and advice are now recorded in a book for teachers to keep by them and to consult year by year. It took many years to write, and it will be many more in active service.

L. F. Ennever
University of Bristol
1974

Acknowledgements

The Project is deeply grateful to its many friends: to the local education authorities who have helped us work in their areas, to those of their staff who, acting as area representatives, have borne the heavy brunt of administering our trials, and to the teachers, heads and wardens who have been generous without stint in working with their children on our materials. The books we have written drew substance from the work they did for us, and it was through their critical appraisal that our materials reached their present form. For guidance, we had our sponsors, our Consultative Committee and, for support, in all our working, the University of Bristol. To all of them, we acknowledge our many debts: their help has been invaluable.

It is a pleasure to acknowledge some further help of special value. Mr L. C. Comber, chairman of the Consultative Committee for the Science 5/13 Project and formerly HM Staff Inspector for Rural Studies read the first draft of *Using the environment*. His comments and suggestions have been of the greatest possible assistance in the work that followed.

Some of the apparatus photographed in Volume 3 has been constructed by Mr W. A. J. Edwards and Mr D. Postill, Kent Education Committee Inspectors. Mr Postill has also checked sections in each book where there is emphasis on mathematical ideas.

Metrication

This has given us a great deal to think about. We have been given much good advice by well-informed friends, and we have consulted many reports by learned bodies. Following the advice and the reports wherever possible we have expressed quantities in metric units with Imperial units afterwards in square brackets if it seemed useful to state them so.

There are, however, some cases to which the recommendations are difficult to apply. For instance we have difficulty with units such as miles per hour (which has statutory force in this country) and with some Imperial units that are still in current use for common commodities and, as far as we know, liable to remain so for some time. In these cases we have tried to use our common sense, and in order to make statements that are both accurate and helpful to teachers we have quoted Imperial measures followed by the approximate metric equivalent in square brackets if it seemed sensible to give them.

Where we have quoted statements made by children or given illustrations that are children's work, we have left unaltered the units in which the children worked—in any case some of these units were arbitrary.

Contents

1	**Introduction**
3	**1 How does the weather change?**
4	Collecting rain
7	Water in other states
8	The changing clouds
9	Changes in visibility
9	Does the wind change?
14	Observing the direction of the wind
18	Measuring temperature
19	Siting a school weather station
20	Records and relationships
21	**2 How do plants and animals change?**
21	Autumn and winter activities
22	Studies of growth and development
27	From early states of development to maturity
33	Interesting life histories
41	Changes in adult plants and animals
42	Seasonal changes—studying deciduous trees
45	Other useful material
47	**3 The changing landscape**
47	Observing the land's surface
49	Looking downwards into the soil
50	Looking backwards in time
53	Following changes with the seasons
53	What is the land made of?
58	The action of other agencies upon the soil: moving and mixing
63	**4 The children's playground as a centre of interest**
65	Beginning with a slide
75	Beginning with a seesaw
78	Beginning with a swing
81	Beginning on things that go round

82	**5 Work with birds**
83	Recognition
84	Counting birds
90	Feeding habits
93	Characteristic movements
98	The shape of birds
98	Nest building and parental care
99	Making sounds
101	**6 Writing about the environment**
101	Personal writing
102	The teacher's influence
103	Freedom of expression
105	Finding the right time
106	Developing an argument
106	Supporting statements with evidence
107	Direct experience helping imagination
109	Developing skill and accuracy
111	**Objectives for children learning science**
119	**Index**

Introduction

This is a book about field studies. It deals with investigations and problems children can discover through their natural interest in their outdoor surroundings. Such first-hand experience, gained from the environment, is the basis of learning, provoking thought, giving children many ideas to share through speech and writing and sending them to books and other secondary sources of information to add to their own findings.

In the countryside there is so much more material of educational value than one book can cover that here there must be selection. We concern ourselves with things that have always interested scientists—natural phenomena that can be investigated through the human senses.

No rigid course with the same material for all is offered, that would fail to satisfy children's individual needs. When children work naturally they respond to the same starting points in different ways and soon become interested in different aspects of a common study. Later, as their development continues, they acquire the ability to make general statements about their experience or, as we usually say 'form concepts', but, here, again, it is through varied experience that each child's understanding of ideas is consolidated and deepened.

Piaget, and others, have shown that children pass through the same stages of intellectual development in acquiring the power of conceptual thought but there is nothing sudden about this maturing, it is something children come to at their own rate with frequent returns to earlier ways of thinking and working when new situations have to be faced. This means that we shall find children, even of the same age, at different stages in the way they learn from their surroundings so teachers must be prepared to vary their influence correspondingly. For these reasons the material in this book is arranged in an order that can be related to children's changing needs as their experience of outdoor investigation increases.

Volume 1 is concerned with the earliest exploration beyond the classroom when children need experience that can sharpen their sensory perception and help them to think about the numerical and spatial aspects of their surroundings.

Usually this would apply to infants but older children, coming to field studies for the first time, will need some practice in early stages of the work before they become ready to deal with studies appropriate for more experienced investigators.

Volume 2 contains many questions and suggestions designed to help children work actively and purposefully on studies in depth. They become ready to do this when they find something of particular interest on which they wish to focus attention.

Volume 3 could serve as an impetus to children's investigation of some major biological ideas and relationships through the design of controlled experiments. They should be able to deal with the reasoning this involves as their capacity for abstract thought develops.

Volume 4 is relevant to fieldwork at all times. It deals with ways and means of providing the facilities, equipment and raw materials children need for all stages of their outdoor investigations and resulting activities on their return to study areas in school.

A book concerned with the countryside should create awareness of the many ways in which living things and environmental conditions affect each other so suggestions for studying these relationships and the consequences of disturbing them have been included. Every future citizen requires this knowledge as a basis for responsible attitudes towards the use of land and natural resources (ie *conservation*) in view of the ever-increasing demands a rising world population and desire for better standards of living will continue to make on the world's finite stores of materials.

Although this book is about children it is not for them, it is a book for teachers and it could not have been written without their help. Many teachers, and in particular some in Derbyshire and Kent, have contributed directly or indirectly to its contents. They have done so by encouraging children to pursue scientific interests, share common experiences and record what seems significant to them. They have collected questions children have asked, described models they have designed and noted suggestions and problems that have absorbed their attention. In this way a large collection of ideas has emerged from children's purposeful activity, guided carefully by thoughtful teachers. This is now available as a source of inspiration from which other teachers can select when children they know, show by their questions and behaviour, that they are near the end of their own ideas and resources and need contact with the greater experience of an interested adult.

We suggest that before reading this second part of *Investigations* teachers should read the first chapter of Part 1 since the general principles discussed there are applicable to the whole of Volume 2.

1 How does the weather change?

In this and the following two chapters we shall be concerned with some of the various ways of helping children become more aware of the dynamic nature of their surroundings: things that change. In weather they will meet a set of conditions that can change rapidly. 'Further outlook unsettled' is a familiar comment from many British weather reports even though we may from time to time enjoy a long hot summer or think a cold spell will never end. Since weather is always there it will be studied in many ways at many different times by primary school children.

Younger children are unlikely to begin with weather as a whole. Conditions that may affect their immediate activities will arouse their greatest interest.

Will the fine weather last until Thursday for our visit to the downs?

Will the wind blow down more conkers than it did yesterday?

When can we begin swimming?

When they have been impressed by something less usual like a very heavy snowfall or torrential rain 'How much?' is a good question to ask them, for it may help them to collect some interesting measurements for comparison with more normal daily observations.

As the more experienced children's records accumulate they will have acquired material that may show interesting patterns of change.

Does the temperature rise or fall when fine weather follows a wet spell?

At what time of the year are we likely to get:

The lowest temperatures?
The heaviest rainfall?
The strongest winds?

Perhaps these children could try to discover whether there is any justification for some of our well-known weather sayings.

Eventually some of the older juniors (ten to eleven years) will want information about different weather conditions affecting one place at the same time. Then they need their own weather station. In developing such a project children may still concentrate on particular aspects of the work, but their combined results are more likely to show any relationships that may exist.

In whatever way and at whatever time children may investigate weather conditions they are likely to become concerned with:

The design of apparatus.
Making improvements to earlier models.
Thinking about scientific ideas that must be taken into account in order to make home-made apparatus work successfully.

Some ways in which these concerns are part of various investigations will now be considered.

Collecting rain

What is the best container for rain? Test various shapes and sizes. Under what conditions should all these vessels be tested? (Heavy and light rain, strong winds.)

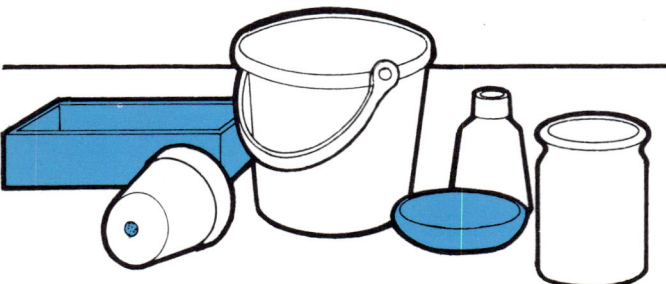

What characteristics are important in making a choice? (Stability, contents visible for measurement.)

Where shall we put the selected container (ie the rain gauge)?

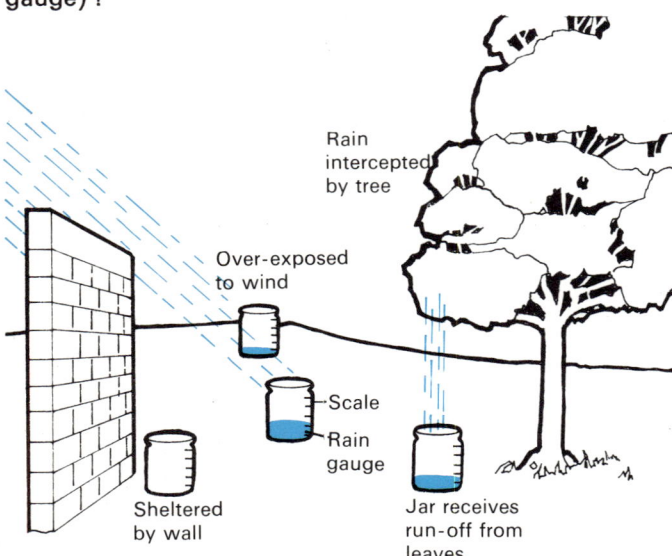

Reject jars containing excessive and very small amounts of water.

How can we compare the amounts of rain collected on different days?

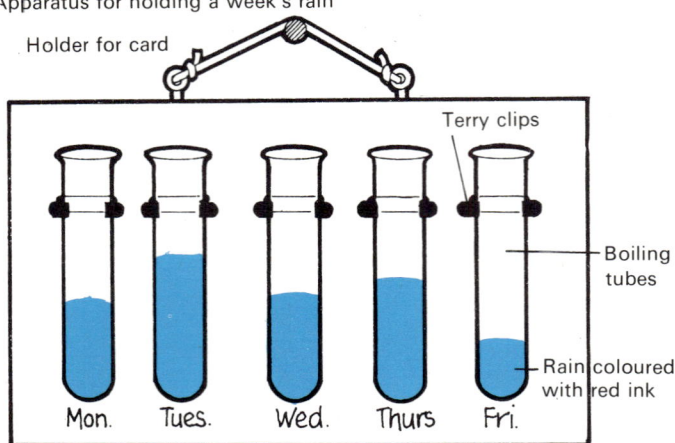

If daily collections of rain are transferred to appropriate tubes, the children will have constructed a model of a block graph representing a week's rainfall in a certain place.

Note that activities involving the transfer of water to vessels of a different shape will be meaningless to children who have not developed an understanding of the conservation of volume. Teachers should therefore check this in discussion before proceeding.

From this it is a short step to the production of a book of records.

Improving the rain gauge
Prevention of evaporation

Puddles and the washing of fabrics in the home corner will have provided some experience of 'drying up' (see Volume 1, pages 16 and 17).

Does 'drying up' affect the contents of the rain gauge?

Half fill the class rain gauge with water. Mark the level and leave it out of doors for twenty-four hours. Repeat when weather conditions are different.

Can water be evaporated from this model?

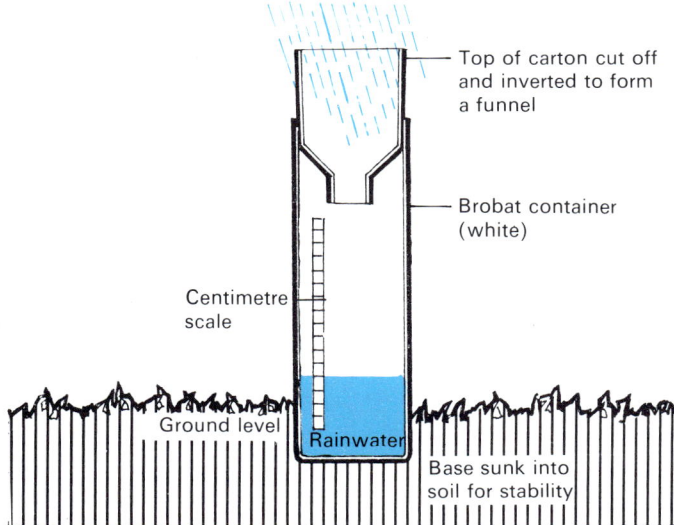

In this apparatus rainwater will be visible as a darker shape through the thin white walls, so its depth can be measured without difficulty. Could this design be further improved so that removal from its position in the soil becomes unnecessary?

Consideration of the risk of raindrops rebounding from the ground into the funnel of the rain gauge

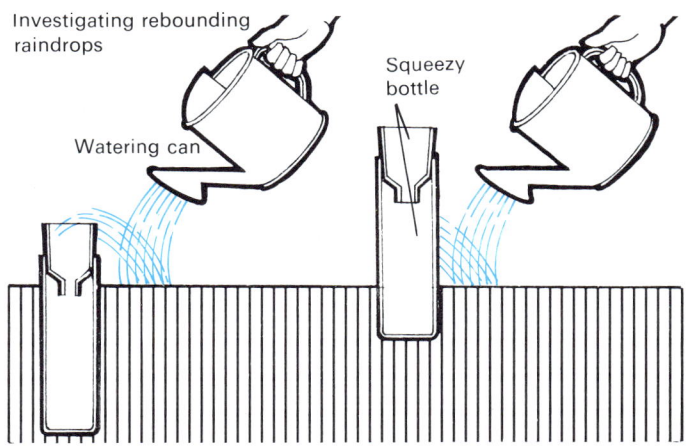

From what type of surfaces do raindrops splash highest?

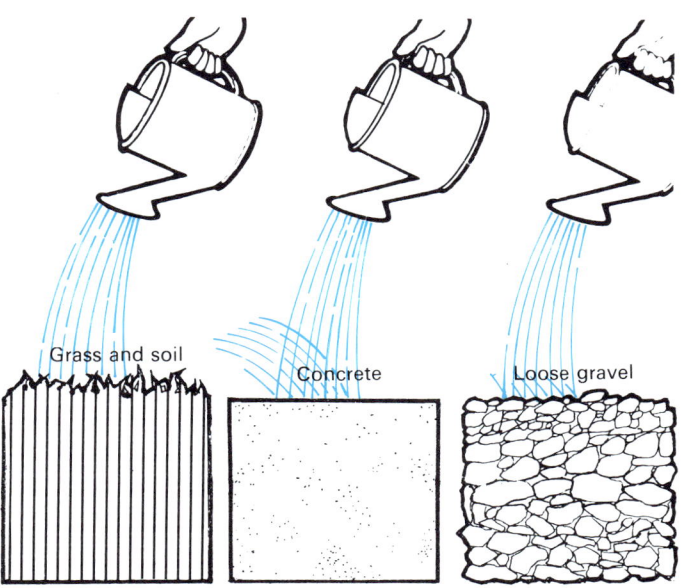

How high must the funnel of the rain gauge be to avoid taking in additional water from splashing?

Note. The standard height of the funnel for rain gauges is accepted as 30 cm above ground level.

A useful rain gauge sufficiently tall to avoid raindrops rebounding from the ground can be made from a 42-cm length of plastic Marley drainpipe with a 10·15-cm (4-in) internal diameter.

Drive it into the ground to a depth of 12 cm. Place a plastic disc over the soil that the pipe encloses. The airtight lid sold with 226-g (8-oz) tins of coffee is exactly the right size for this purpose.

Stand a glass or plastic bottle on the plastic disc as shown in the diagram. If rain is caught in it the outer casing need not be removed from the ground. Finally, fit a plastic funnel of 10·15-cm (4-in) diameter across the pipe so that its stem leads into the collecting bottle.

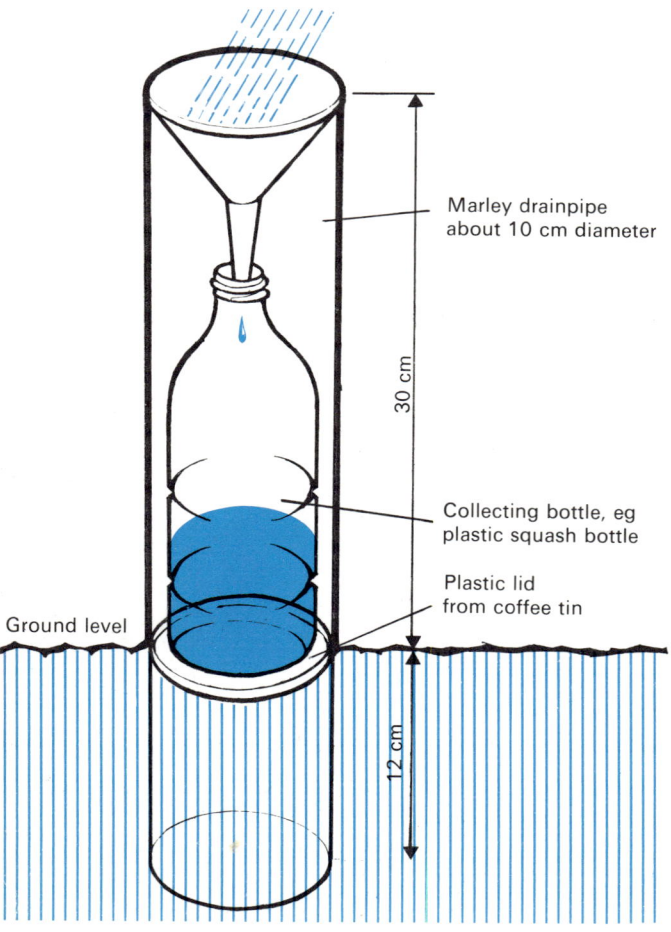

What information can these home-made rain gauges provide?

This must be considered very carefully with children to ensure against false claims.

In these vessels children collect for equal periods of time rain that would have fallen on ground approximately equal in area to the mouth of an open collecting jar or funnel.

When rain is directed into an inner vessel of smaller diameter than the wide end of the funnel, its depth will increase. Therefore, the inner vessel must be calibrated so that the depth its contents would assume in a container of the same diameter as the funnel, can be read directly.

This can most easily be done by transferring to the inner collecting bottle quantities of water 10 mm in depth from a circular shallow tin or petri dish of the same diameter as the funnel. As each quantity is added mark the new level on the side of the bottle. From the scale produced in this way the depth of rain in the gauge can be read in one-centimetre units.

Records of rainfall in sufficient number can provide children with evidence of:

The wettest day of the month.
The month that had most rainy days.
When no rain fell.
Thursday being twice or half as wet as Wednesday.

But such statements only apply to the place where the rain gauge stood.

By placing similar home-made rain gauges in different parts of the school field or garden for the same periods of time and comparing their contents, children can discover whether the contents of the vessel in regular use is likely to be representative of the rain also falling over the surrounding area. (This might be a good introduction to the technique of sampling.) Older children wishing to exchange records with schools in other parts of the country or world may find some advantage in using a commercial rain gauge. For further details about the use of this see Volume 3 Part 2, page 33.

Water in other states

Appropriate weather conditions may arouse children's curiosity about water in different forms, such as:

Snowflakes, (groups of interlocked ice crystals).
Hailstones, (water frozen into pellets of ice).
Frost, (frozen dew).

They are likely to be less interested in the way these things are formed than in discovering what they are like or how they can be changed.

Investigations
1. Place a snowflake or hailstone on a dark background, and observe with a stereomicroscope. How does it change?

2. Squeeze lumps of snow tightly.

3. Place some water in the freezing box of a refrigerator and note the time it takes it to become ice. Repeat, using the same quantity of water in which salt has been dissolved.

4. Stand a tightly corked medicine bottle full of water in an empty bucket out of doors when a sharp frost is expected. Leave overnight. (Relate this to what happens when pipes burst.)

5. Calculate the volume of a cube of ice from the refrigerator. Measure the volume of water produced when it melts.

6. Place cubes of ice in water and note their proportions above and below the water surface. (Relate this to icebergs.)

7. Use a long stick to measure the depth of snow in various parts of the school grounds. Try to discover why the depths differ. (One of the reasons is drifting in relation to wind direction and barriers.)

The magnified structure of a hailstone
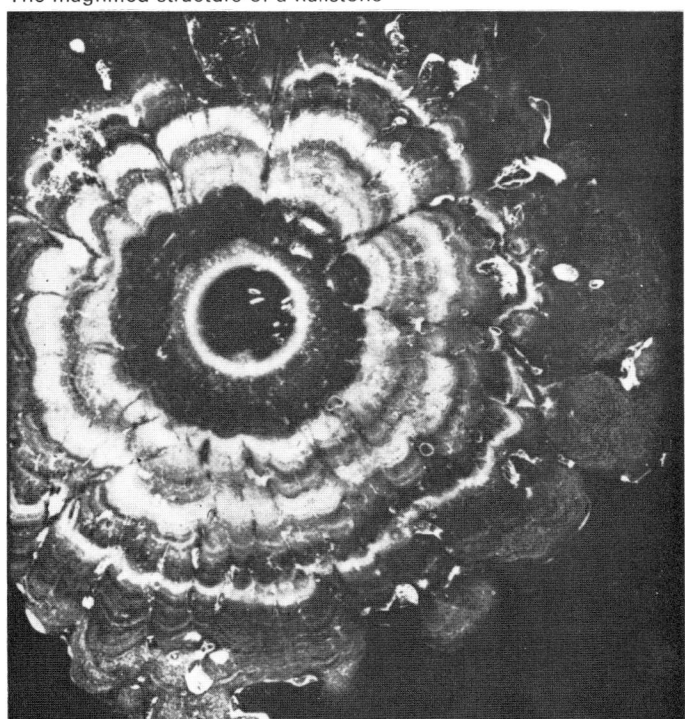

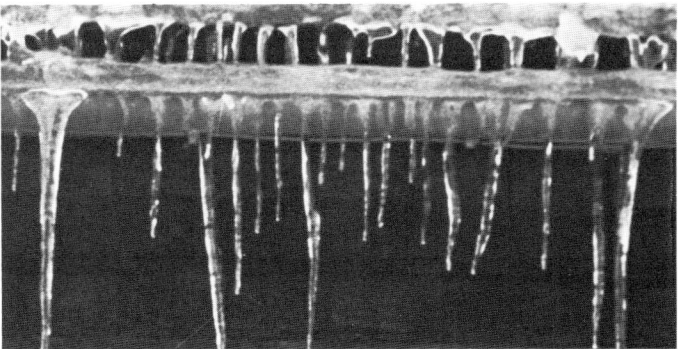

The changing clouds

The movements of clouds can best be observed with the aid of a home-made reflector.

Make this by inserting a sheet of black card or paper beneath the glass of an old picture frame.

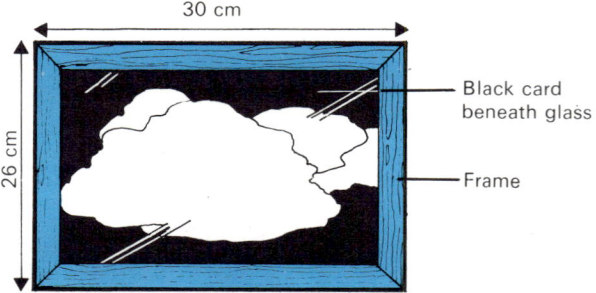

Children will soon discover that areas of sky visible in this apparatus are much larger than the actual area of the reflector. Place the reflector flat on the ground beneath a low branch of a tree. Measure the length of the reflection and compare its length with that of the actual branch. This is good experience of reduction to scale.

Are things higher than the branch still further reduced in size in the reflector? Try to discover some evidence in support of such an idea.

Investigations of clouds

With the aid of reference books try to name some of the cloud forms that pass across the reflector.

Do some clouds appear to be higher in the sky than others?
Do different types of cloud move at different rates?
Does the size of a cloud make any difference to its rate of movement?
Do clouds move faster when the wind is strong?
Does the direction in which the wind blows affect clouds?
Do rainy days seem to go with certain types of cloud?
What kinds of clouds are most frequently seen on fine days?

Different cloud formations

Changes in visibility

Children observing landscape will soon find that the number of conspicuous landmarks that can be seen and recognised at different times will vary.

They will need a scale of visibility in order to compare such observations. Here is how to make a scale.

Look at the surrounding countryside from an upper window or flat part of the school roof.
Choose four conspicuous landmarks at distances of 1, 2, 4, and 8 kilometres from the building as the crow flies. Give each a letter, beginning with the nearest object. Visibility from the school viewpoint can then be described by the letter corresponding to the most distant of these landmarks at the time of observation.

Here is an example of a scale of this sort.

Landmark	Distance from viewpoint in km	Visibility sign and description
School gate	0·5	A (very poor)
Lombardy poplar tree	1·0	B (poor)
St Mark's church steeple	2·0	C (moderate)
Factory chimney	4·0	D (good)
Radar mast	8·0	E (very good)

When the visibility is C, for example, the school gate and poplar tree will be even more easily seen than the church steeple. But the factory chimney and radar mast will not be recognisable.

To estimate visibility when on an expedition, note the most conspicuous landmark that can be seen from a convenient viewpoint. On return to school use a map measurer or the map scale to determine the distance between this landmark and the viewpoint.

The letter on the scale corresponding to that distance will provide the required estimate of visibility.

Does the wind change?

Wind is invisible, so children must gain many of their ideas about it by observing its effect on other things.

Measuring the force exerted by the wind
Make some air move by pushing it out of the carton. Give a name to what can be felt.

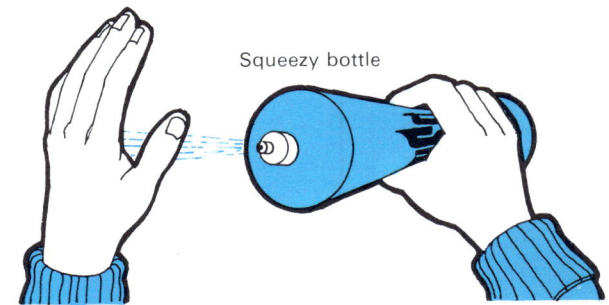
Squeezy bottle

When air moves it will push against things that happen to be in its way and drive them along if they are light.

Play the party game of 'Flip the Kipper'. This can be a race in which wind is used to drive the paper fish along.

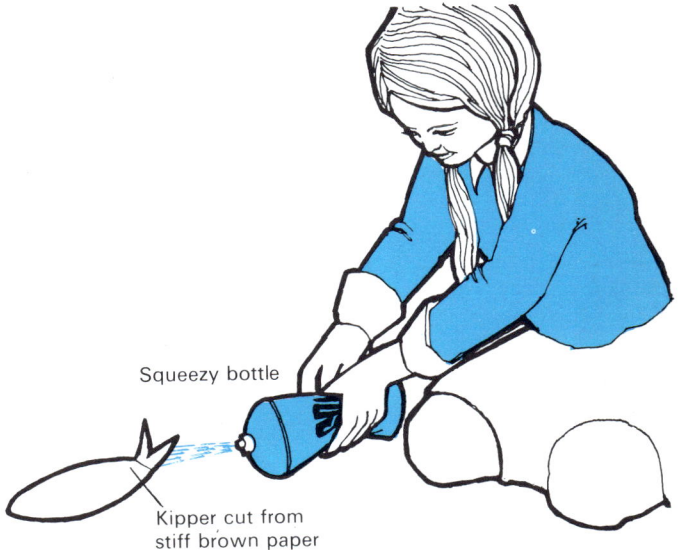
Squeezy bottle
Kipper cut from stiff brown paper

When Jeanette and Angela flew their home-made kites on a windy day they soon discovered that they had to pull to hold on to the string as the wind pushed against their kites. The wind and the girls were exerting force in opposite directions. Here are the poems they wrote when they returned to their classroom.

Kites
Kites kites floating through the sky
Big kites soaring through the air
Racing through the air come the kites
I hold the string tightly — a good grip I've got
The wind is pushing, the kites are flying
The wind is blowing — I am still holding the string.

Jeanette Robinson, aged seven years.

My kite in the sky
My kite is in the sky
Oh how that wind is trying
The wind wants my kite
Oh that wild wind
My kite swoops in the wind
And it darts from place to place.
In the sky up, up
My kite flies
Swaying from side to side
Then it lashes against the wind
I grip on my hand as tightly as I can
Soaring in the sky my kite shines bright
Swiftly it sways in the sky
Then I pull it down to the ground.

Angela Turner, aged eight years.

Other children can find out how to make kites from *Make and Find Out,* Books 1 and 4 by K. Geary (Macmillan, 1970).

Does the wind exert more force on certain days?
This idea might be tested by attaching a dynamometer to the string of the same kite while flying it on different days and comparing readings on the scale. The extension of a rubber band could be used instead of a dynamometer.

The faster things move the harder they push against things in their path.

An analogy might be used to help children to relate the ideas involved in this statement to the wind.

Arrange some situations in which a ball-bearing travels down a sloping track at different speeds and then comes in contact with a glass marble. When is this marble moved the greatest distance?

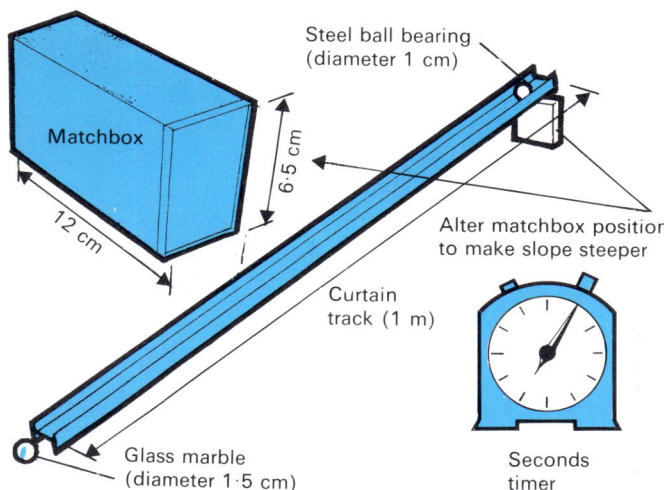

Material seen moving	Wind description	Wind strength in numerical form
None	Calm	0
Tissue paper	Light	1
Tissue paper + Ribbon	Moderate	2
Tissue paper + Ribbon + Nail	Fresh	3

When children have had sufficient experience of this to enable them to realise that the ball-bearing pushes against the marble harder and harder as its speed increases, they can be asked to speculate about the kind of wind that causes the most movement of other things.

If we can find ways of comparing what the wind moves at different times we shall also know more about the speed with which it is moving at these same times and the force it is exerting.

Here are some suggestions for apparatus and examples of scales in arbitrary units that might be devised for use with them.

Leonardo da Vinci was the first to make an indicator of the type (seen below). It gives more precise arbitrary measurements of changes in the wind's strength than the previous model.

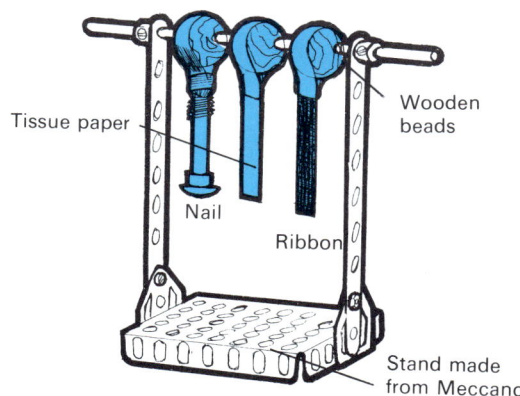

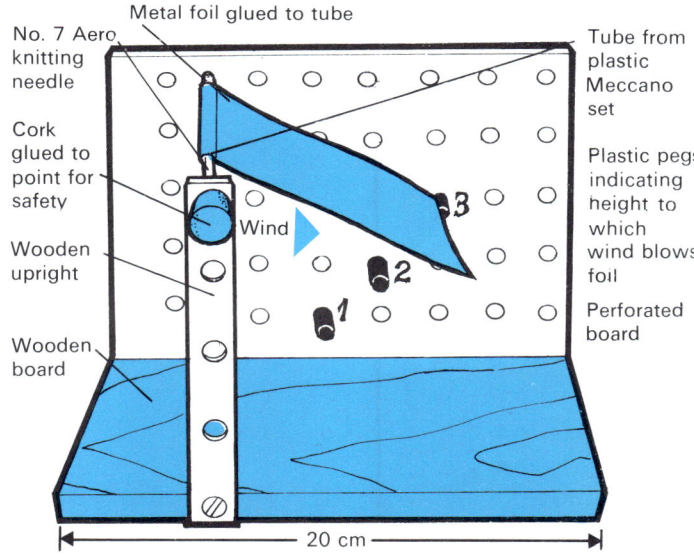

Scale in arbitrary units:
0 → calm
1 → light wind
2 → moderate wind
3 → fresh wind
4 → strong wind

11

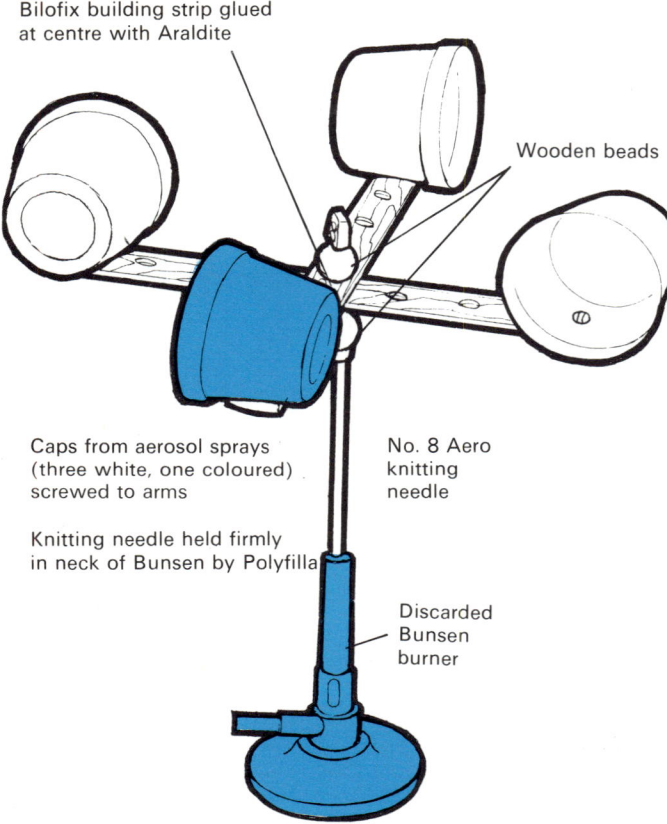

An anemometer

Bilofix building strip glued at centre with Araldite

Wooden beads

Caps from aerosol sprays (three white, one coloured) screwed to arms

No. 8 Aero knitting needle

Knitting needle held firmly in neck of Bunsen by Polyfilla

Discarded Bunsen burner

This instrument must be fixed firmly to the top of a pole or wall to receive the effects of the wind.

The greater the force of the wind the faster the cups rotate. Here is a scale for the anemometer.

No. of turns in 10 seconds	Wind	Wind strength in numerical form
No movement	Calm	0
1–3	Light	1
4–6	Moderate	2
7–9	Fresh	3
9–12	Strong	4

If children have difficulty in getting their anemometers to work successfully, the opportunity is provided for discussing the following scientific ideas.

1. Reduction of friction
If the arms do not revolve smoothly:
Examine the size of the central hole—is it large enough?
Note that the arms will tilt if it is too large.
Is the wood surrounding the hole smooth where it is in contact with the knitting needle?
Is the distance between the beads above and below the arms sufficient to allow free movement?
Is movement aided by lubricating the edges of the central hole with Vaseline?
The curved surfaces of the beads also reduce friction.

2. Opposing forces
A gentle breeze may have no effect on the anemometer. Wind speed must be sufficient to give the cups stronger pushes than any opposing forces affecting them and also to counteract any resistance due to friction.

3. The number of revolutions
Does ability to count the revolutions of the coloured cup at high wind speeds depend on the length of the arms of the instrument?

Calibrating
So far we have considered arbitrary scales that will give children information about the wind when they use their own instruments, but they cannot compare these findings with any made elsewhere unless a standard scale is used.

In 1805 Admiral Sir Francis Beaufort constructed a scale in which he related the speed of wind, and hence the force it can exert, to its power to move sailing ships. Today, the wind's varying speed and force are related to internationally agreed signs of movement of objects on land.

If children use the Beaufort scale (as shown on the right) to make a rough calibration of their own anemometers, they should:

Take note of the kind of things being moved by the wind.

Read off the force this represents on the Beaufort Scale.

BEAUFORT WIND SCALE

ASHORE	DEFINITION	SIGN	FORCE	WIND
	SMOKE RISES VERTICALLY	⊙	0	CALM
	WIND DIRECTION IS SHOWN BY SMOKE DRIFT BUT NOT BY VANES	→	1	LIGHT AIR
	THE WIND IS FELT ON THE FACE: LEAVES RUSTLE VANES MOVE IN THE WIND	⇀	2	LIGHT BREEZE
	A LIGHT FLAG WOULD BE EXTENDED BY THE WIND: LEAVES AND SMALL TWIGS WOULD BE IN CONSTANT MOTION	⇛→	3	GENTLE BREEZE
	DUST IS RAISED AND LOOSE PAPER BLOWS ABOUT ON SHORE SMALL BRANCHES ARE MOVED	⇛⇛→	4	MODERATE BREEZE
	SMALL TREES IN LEAF BEGIN TO SWAY: CRESTED WAVELETS FORM ON INLAND WATERS	⇛⇛→	5	FRESH BREEZE
	LARGE TREE BRANCHES WOULD BE SET IN MOTION: THERE WOULD BE A WHISTLING IN THE TELEGRAPH WIRES. UMBRELLAS DIFFICULT	⇛⇛→	6	STRONG BREEZE
	WHOLE TREES ARE IN MOTION. SOME INCONVENIENCE FELT WHEN WALKING	⇛⇛→	7	HIGH WIND
	IN WHICH THE TWIGS ARE BROKEN OFF TREES AND PROGRESS IS IMPEDED	⇛⇛⇛→	8	FRESH GALE
	SLIGHT STRUCTURAL DAMAGE WOULD BE OCCASIONED AND CHIMNEY POTS AND SLATES MIGHT FLY	⇛⇛⇛→	9	STRONG GALE
	THERE IS CONSIDERABLE STRUCTURAL DAMAGE AND WHOLE TREES ARE BEING UPROOTED	⇛⇛⇛→	10	WHOLE GALE
	SUCH WIND IS FORTUNATELY RARELY EXPERIENCED FOR IT CAUSES WIDESPREAD DAMAGE	⇛⇛⇛→	11	STORM
	———————	⇛⇛⇛→	12	HURRICANE

Count the number of turns of the coloured cup on the anemometer in 10 seconds in these conditions.

By repeating this procedure at different times they will collect the information they require.

When this type of scale is being constructed, the standard signs for wind force could be introduced.

The number of projections on the tails of the arrows correspond to the figure describing the wind force.

A ventimeter

Older children can make a more exact calibration of their anemometers with a yachtsman's ventimeter. This instrument (obtainable from Captain O. M. Watts Ltd, 49 Albemarle Street, London W1) gives direct readings of wind speeds.

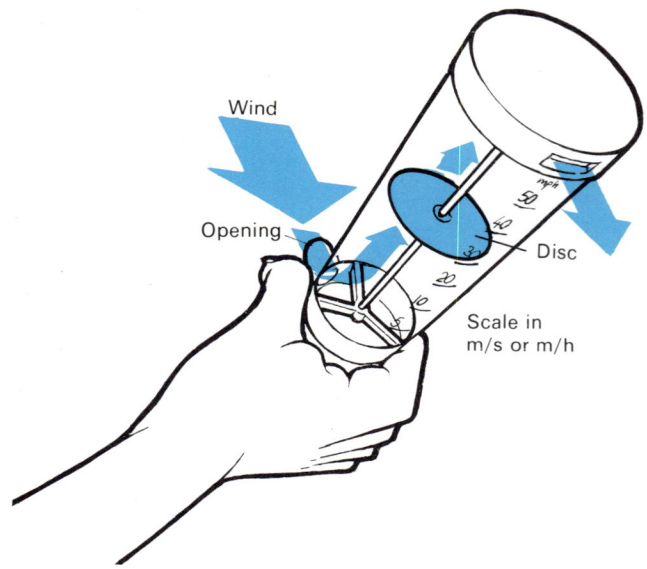

Hold the gauge at eye level with the opening facing the wind. As the wind enters the instrument it will lift the disc. Its position in relation to the scale on the side of the instrument gives the wind speed (and its force). Children can find the number of turns made by the coloured cup of their anemometers in 10 seconds at this speed and again construct a scale similar to that given on page 12, but with the actual wind speeds in metres per second occupying the third column of the table.

Other investigations

In addition to recording daily changes in the strength of the wind, changes in the force it exerts in different places at the same time can be investigated, for example:

Horizontally; on the sheltered and exposed side of a hedge or wall, in the middle of a field, under trees.
Vertically; halfway up a hill, at the top of a hill, from the base and top of a wall.

Observing the direction of the wind

An idea that must always be associated with movement is direction.

Try to watch bubbles, balloons, birds, traffic or boats.
Where are they coming from?
What are they going towards?

For daily observation of wind direction children need things that can be moved by wind but not blown away.

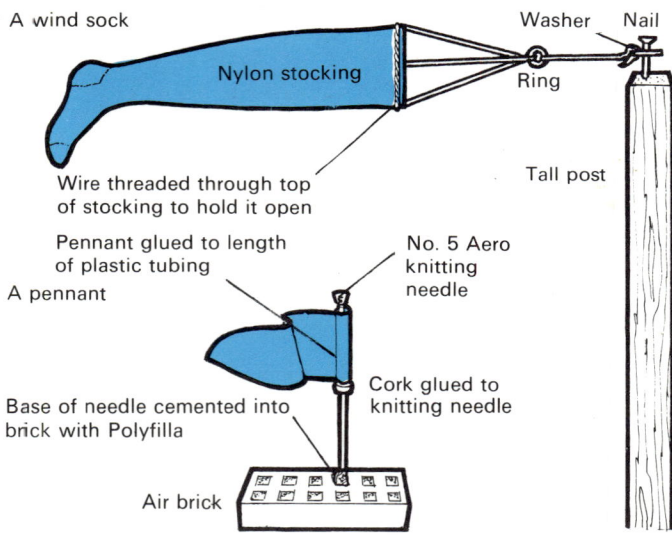

If some children would like to make wind socks like those used on airfields, they should first make a pattern out of newspaper. They will discover that the best shape for this is a cone.

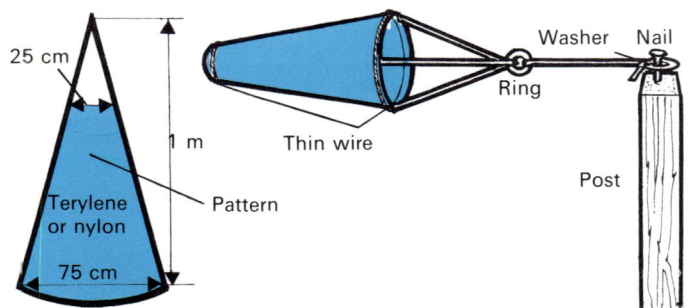

Children's first descriptions of direction will be made by pointing, or relating moving objects to conspicuous landmarks, for example:

'The thrush flew to the TV aerial.'
'The boat is going further and further away from the lighthouse.'
'The wind is coming from where I am facing.'

These comments can only apply to particular places. So they will not do for comparisons.

The points of the compass
Just as children need, in due course, to compare different distances and masses with standard units, so they will find they need a standard way of referring to directions. This is the time for experience designed to develop understanding of the points of the compass.

Shadow stick

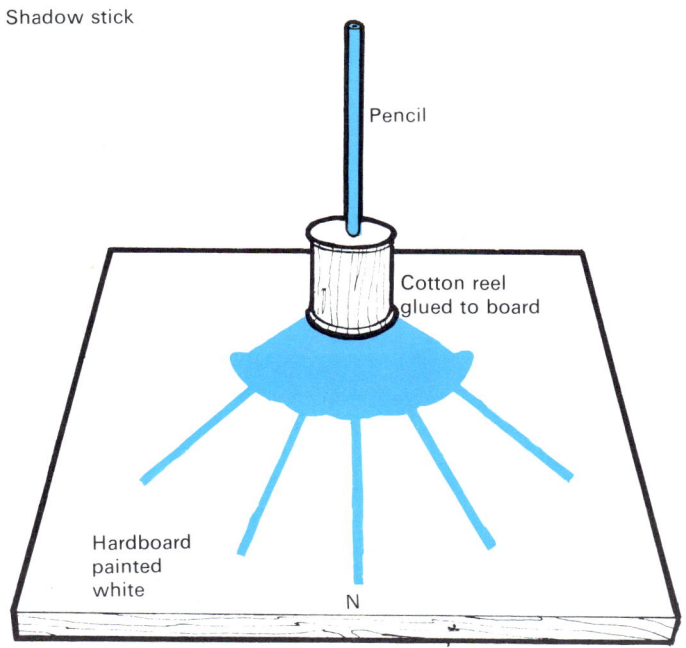

Finding north

At noon each day draw a line on the playground coinciding with the shadow cast by the stick.

The shadow points in the same direction at noon each day because the sun which causes it is also in approximately the same place every day.

It will help children if these directions, which are called compass directions, can be marked on the playground surface with white road paint. This method for finding north could be used anywhere in the northern part of the world when the sun is shining. A method for dull days is also needed, for instance, the compass can be used.

15

At midday on sunny days place a large compass on the stick's shadow. In what direction does the needle lie? Children can be shown how to line up a compass correctly by turning it gently so that north on the white card lies beneath the end of the needle pointing to the northern end of the shadow.

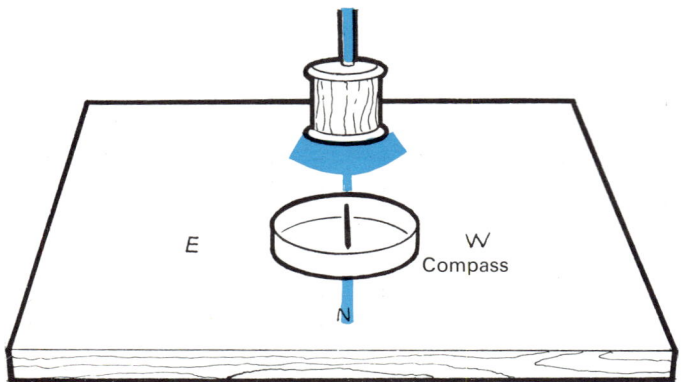

At this stage more experience with magnets is also relevant.

Mark the north-seeking pole on all magnets used.

Place small bar magnets on flat corks floating in water. In what direction do they lie?

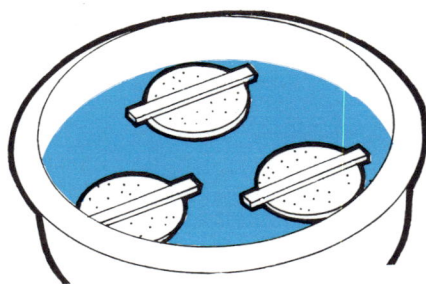

Suspend a bar magnet in a sling of paper or cotton material.

It is necessary to use nylon thread as this is untwisted and therefore will not interfere with the magnet's movements.

In what direction does it come to rest? More than one magnet should be tested in this device.

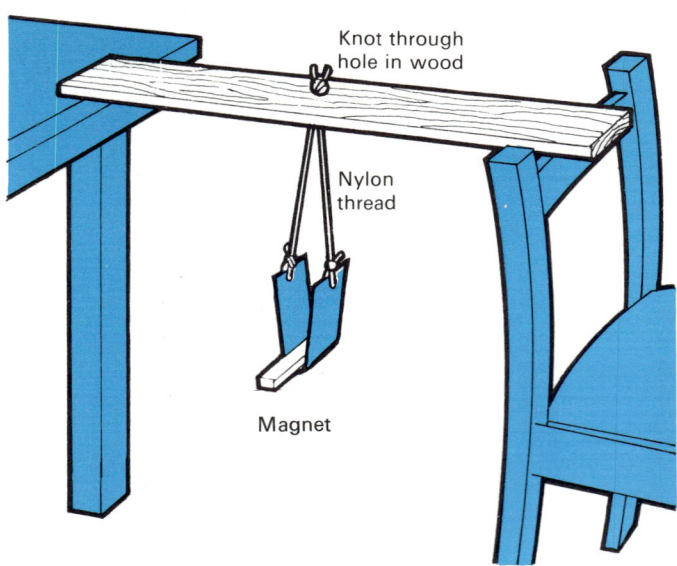

Does the north-seeking pole of the magnet in each test lie in the same direction as the northern end of the shadow on the playground? (See page 15.)

Some children may like to make a compass. For directions see A. James, *Simple Science Experiments*, page 102, (Schofield & Sims, 1964).

Then children should use the compass directions they know for the following purposes:

1. To describe the behaviour of pennants and wind sleeves; the direction of the wind moving these indicators (ie where the wind comes from); the position of landmarks seen during outdoor expeditions.

Note that directions intermediate between the four cardinal points can be given when required.

2. To give directions for other children to follow. 'Walk 20 paces north from the sundial, turn east and continue for 10 paces, now face south and walk 50 paces, then walk 10 paces to the west. Where is your position in relation to the sundial?'

3. In the construction of models indicating wind direction.

Some suggestions for wind vanes

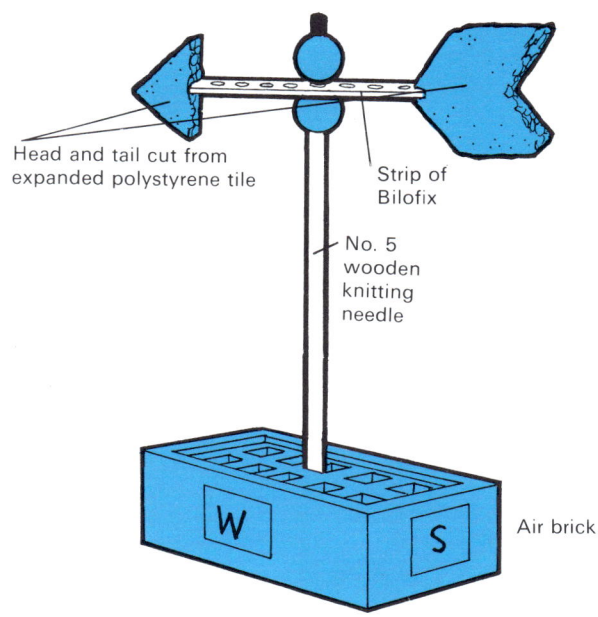

Head and tail cut from expanded polystyrene tile
Strip of Bilofix
No. 5 wooden knitting needle
Air brick

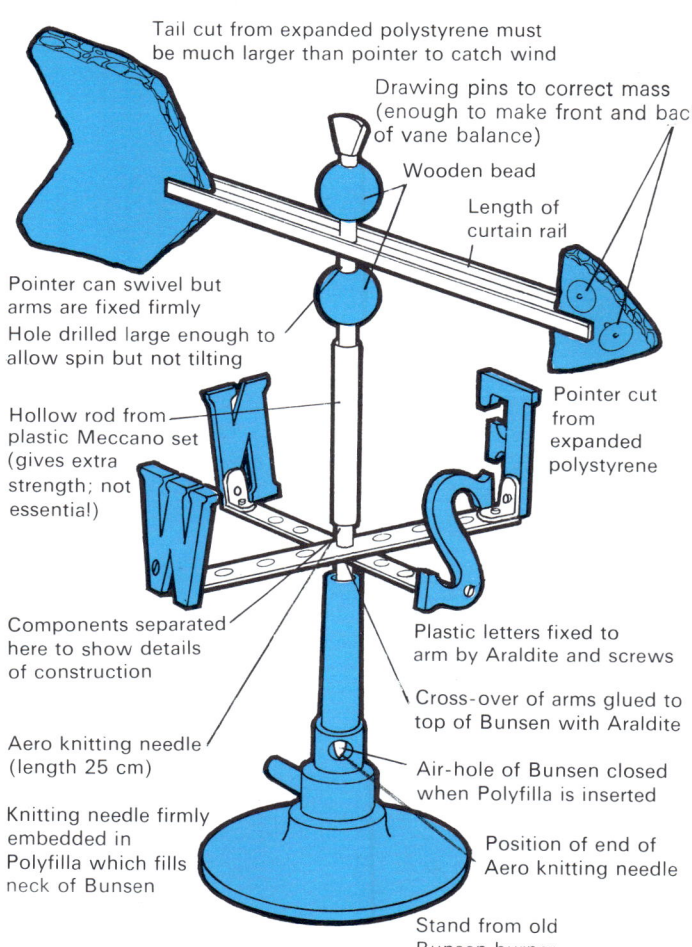

Tail cut from expanded polystyrene must be much larger than pointer to catch wind
Drawing pins to correct mass (enough to make front and back of vane balance)
Wooden bead
Length of curtain rail
Pointer can swivel but arms are fixed firmly
Hole drilled large enough to allow spin but not tilting
Hollow rod from plastic Meccano set (gives extra strength; not essential!)
Pointer cut from expanded polystyrene
Components separated here to show details of construction
Plastic letters fixed to arm by Araldite and screws
Aero knitting needle (length 25 cm)
Cross-over of arms glued to top of Bunsen with Araldite
Air-hole of Bunsen closed when Polyfilla is inserted
Knitting needle firmly embedded in Polyfilla which fills neck of Bunsen
Position of end of Aero knitting needle
Stand from old Bunsen burner

The second construction shown on the right requires considerable manipulative skill and therefore would present older children with a challenge.

Getting models like this to work gives further opportunities for discussion and testing. For example, trying out arrowheads and tailpieces in various sizes may result in the discovery that the tailpiece needs to be considerably larger than the arrowhead. The two arms of the vane must also be in balance if a biased response to a particular wind direction is to be avoided. Easy spinning depends on the reduction of friction.

While these vanes can indicate changes in wind direction, they can also be used for collecting data to show whether there is a most frequent direction in which the wind blows. A prevailing wind will have more influence on a district than a very strong wind on a single day, although this may cause considerable damage at the time. Children should look out for trees affected by a prevailing wind.

Observations of direction can be recorded on a wind rose as shown on the right.

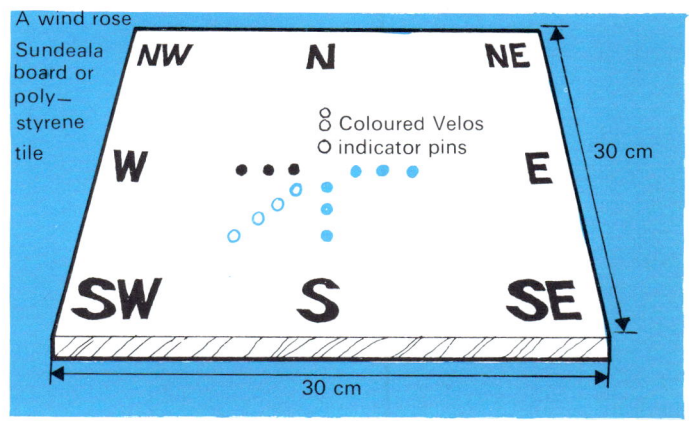

A wind rose
Sundeala board or polystyrene tile
● Coloured Velos
○ indicator pins
30 cm
30 cm

Books containing good ideas for home-made apparatus
Catherall, E. A., and Holt, P. N., *Weather, Working With Series,* Bailey Bros., 1964.
Geary, K., *Make and Find Out,* Macmillan, 1970.
James, A., *Simple Science Experiments,* Schofield & Sims, 1964.
Nuffield *Junior Science Apparatus,* Collins, 1967.
UNESCO, *Source Book for Science Teaching,* HMSO, 1970.

Other activities for older juniors
Try to find north at night by looking for the Pole Star. This star is almost directly above the North Pole, so it can always be found in the same position in the sky, while other groups of stars will be found in different positions during the year owing to the Earth's movement round the sun.

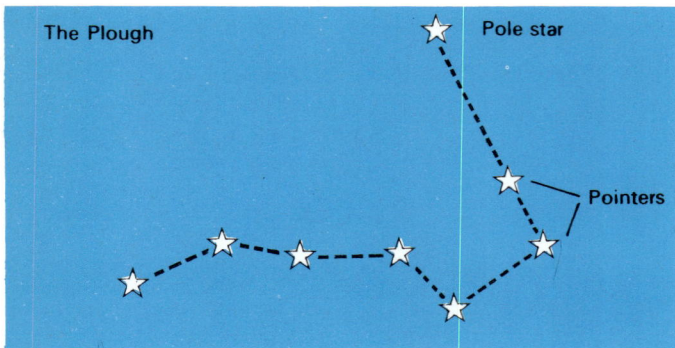

In which direction should you look to see the moon rise?
In which directions do land and sea breezes blow?
What can you find out about trade winds, the doldrums, a monsoon?

Measuring temperature

Heat waves, illness, cooking or a chance to examine different types of thermometer may make children interested in changes of temperature.

What is our normal temperature?
What is our classroom temperature? Will this do for the locust's cage?
What is the temperature of the water in our tropical aquarium?
To what temperature must the water rise before we can use our swimming pool?
At what temperature do the plants in our school pond begin to grow?
Is there any way of measuring the temperature of the soil where we set our seeds yesterday?
What is the temperature of the water under the ice in our school pond?
What is the boiling point of water?
What does 'below zero' mean?
What is the difference between heat and temperature?

Understanding thermometers
Although at this stage children will not make their own thermometers, they do need experience that will help them to understand how they work.

Arrange a flat-bottomed flask and glass tubing as shown. Completely fill the flask with water which has been coloured with crystals of potassium permanganate. Stand it in a bowl of hot water.

What happens to the water in the flask as it becomes warm? (It needs more room.)

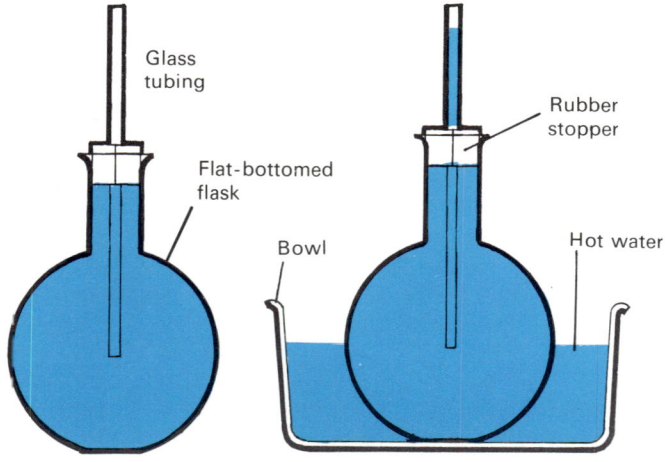

Does the size and shape of container and the diameter of the tube make any difference to the movement of the water when it is heated in this way?

It might be interesting to test some of the following equipment.

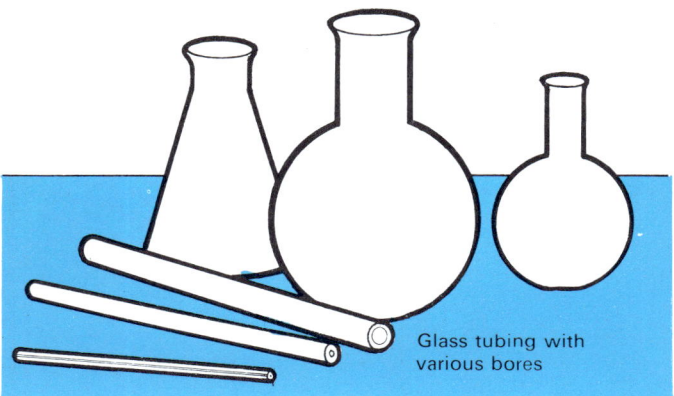

Glass tubing with various bores

Now children can be encouraged to examine their classroom thermometer and some chemical thermometers carefully and make measurements of the bulb, the column of liquid, etc.

What liquids are used in these thermometers?
What is a degree Celsius?

Make comparisons of the temperature of the air at 9.00 am and 4.00 pm each day:

In the classroom.
Out of doors in a sunny place.
Out of doors in a shady place.

Are the temperature readings affected by the position of the thermometers?

Compare the readings of two similar thermometers at the same time each day: one of them hanging to allow circulation of air around its bulb; the other lying flat on a surface.

Note that the maximum and minimum thermometer (often called Six's thermometer after the man who devised it) is a very useful instrument for relating daily temperatures to the growth of living things. If some children become interested in doing this, more information about this thermometer can be found in Volume 3 Part 2, page 38.

Siting a school weather station

Finding a good place for the weather station

In the course of all this work children should use similar home-made instruments in different parts of the school grounds. They should often discover that differences in environmental conditions affect them — sunshine or shade, exposure or shelter, height from the ground, etc. It is therefore obvious that a standard way of exposing meteorological instruments must be agreed if the information they give is to be comparable with that from other places.

A search for information about standard conditions may lead children to reference books and visual materials:
L. P. Smith, *Weathercraft*, Blandford 1964.

Slides and film strip:
Diana Wyllie Ltd (3 Park Road, London NW1), *Running a School Weather Station, Part A, Instruments and Observation.*

They might also correspond with the Royal Meteorological Society (49 Cromwell Road, London, SW7). (See Volume 4, page 32 for further information.)

Records and relationships

Here is an example of the type of chart children dealing with different observations might produce.

It should be drawn on 1-cm squared graph paper.

If all the available data can be seen at the same time there is a better chance of relationships becoming obvious.

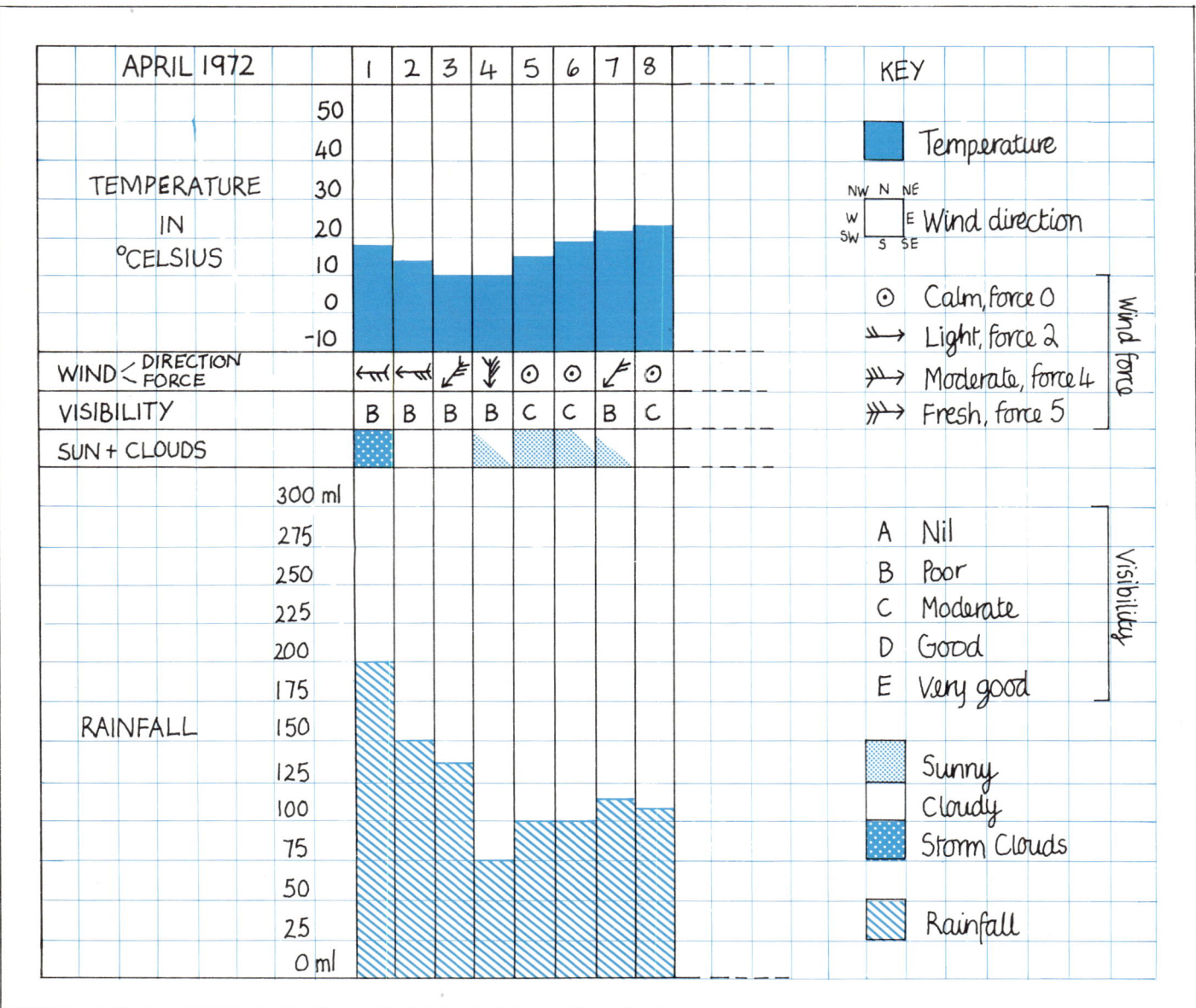

2 How do plants and animals change?

We can expect most discoveries about the ways in which living things change to be made during the spring and summer months when warmer weather and longer hours of daylight speed up growth and cause many creatures to become more active. But some of the things children enjoy doing in autumn and winter can provide a very good introduction to this topic.

Autumn and winter activities

Collecting fruits and seeds (August to November)
The children who do this will have many different things to plant in the following spring.

For berries and tree fruits look in hedgerows and woodland.

Obtain seeds from wild and cultivated plants by tying waterproof Cellophane bags over fruiting heads. Remove these when the fruits have split or shed their seeds into the bags in other ways.

Pips and stones from apples, plums, melons, avocado pears and citrus fruits can be extracted from fruit used in the children's homes.

Seeds should be stored in boxes in separate labelled envelopes and kept cool and dry.

Preparing seed beds and garden plots for the spring sowing (October)
Uproot plants remaining from the previous season. Turn over the soil and remove large stones and pieces of root. If possible fork in some compost or fertiliser. Why should this work be done before the autumn frosts come?

Looking for signs of spring (January to March)
This is a good outdoor investigation for the early months of the year.

Class 3's bulletin board		
Date	Our discoveries	Observers
1974		
16 January	Snowdrops are in bloom in the park	Mary H.
21 January	I saw some long, yellow hazel catkins	John C.
24 January	The winter aconites on our rockery are open	Sheila T.
12 February	I found some coltsfoot in Tubbs Lane	Mark W.
18 February	Today a blackbird in my garden was carrying a twig in its beak	John C.

If children compare observations like these with their weather records they may discover some interesting relationships.

Other children with previous experience of contributing to a class chart may find more interest in keeping and illustrating their own diaries or working with a few others to produce a journal for the school library which can be used for comparison with records of other years. As an illustration of the value of such efforts, extracts from Charles Darwin's journal *The Voyage of the Beagle* or Gilbert White's *Natural History of Selborne* might be read.

Examining large seeds and buds (February)
This is a good thing to do when the weather is unsuitable for outdoor work.

Some seeds that might be examined are: broad bean, pea, horse chestnut, sycamore, acorn, sunflower.

Soak seeds overnight. What changes does this cause?
Carefully peel off the outer skin and examine both surfaces. Is this layer waterproof?
Carefully separate the inner parts. How many different things can be found?
What takes up most space in the seed?

Here are some buds that might be investigated:
Brussels sprouts, lettuce, beech, horse chestnut.

Begin by measuring the bud's length and width.
Then from the outside remove the leaves and arrange them in sequence.
These investigations should help children to realise how much is packed within the small spaces of buds before they start to grow larger in spring.

Providing resources
When children collect living things for further study they must be well housed and maintained.

Here is an estimate the children and their teacher might make of things likely to be needed for this purpose:

Plastic bags and boxes for transport of living material to school.
Containers to hold growing plants.
Tools for cultivating outdoor plots.
Cages for small animals.
Raw materials for making animals' living quarters.
Tools, screws and nails.
Containers for aquatic material.
Holders for food and drinking water.
Equipment for lifting creatures and separating small parts of plants.
Aids to magnification.
Labels for marking growth, noting dates, etc.

This equipment should be gathered ready for the growing season and arranged on open shelving in a resources area.

Studies of growth and development

There is no doubt that children develop the greatest interest in this work when they grow and rear their own specimens. This individual approach brings together a wide range of living things that can then be compared for common patterns of development.

Beginning with seeds
The children's first job will be to make use of available resources to set up conditions in which the seeds they have chosen from the autumn collection can germinate, that is, continue their growth. They should try to do this at the same time in two places with similar sets of seeds:

1. Out of doors in seed beds and plots already prepared, or in window boxes or tubs, when there is no school garden.

2. In school, where it should be possible to devise some **arrangements** whereby all parts of developing seeds are visible. Here are some suggestions.

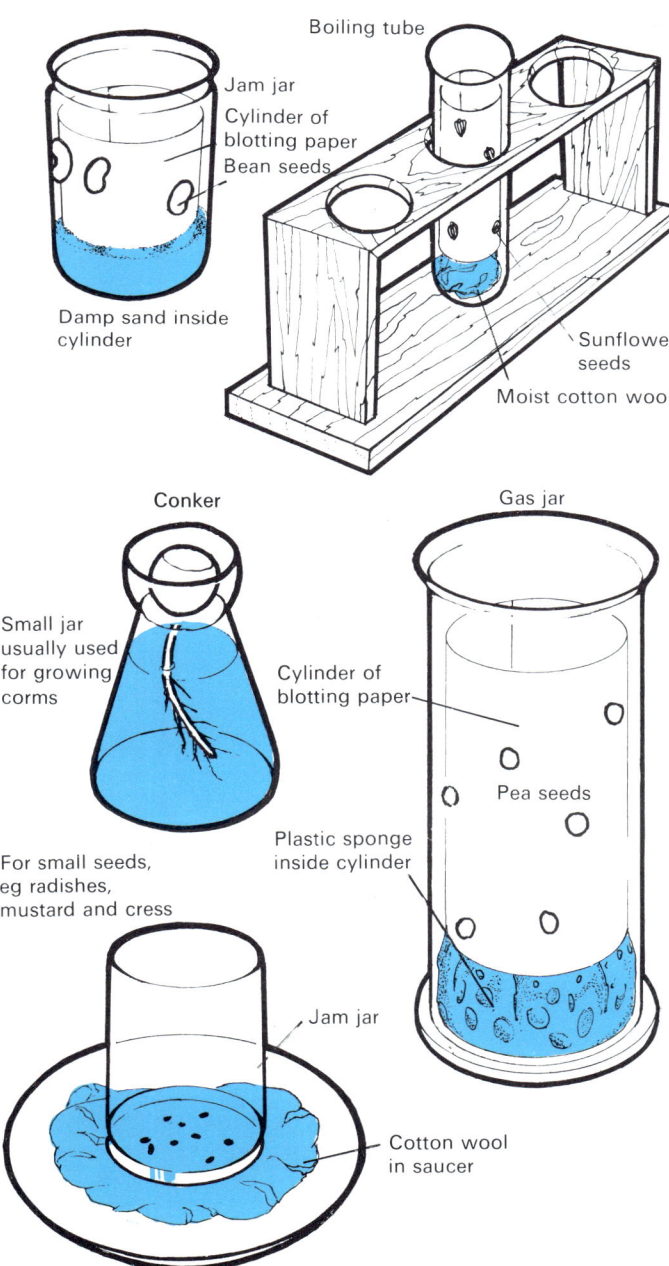

The following arrangement is very satisfactory when it is necessary to observe changes in seeds in relation to the substrate in which they are growing.

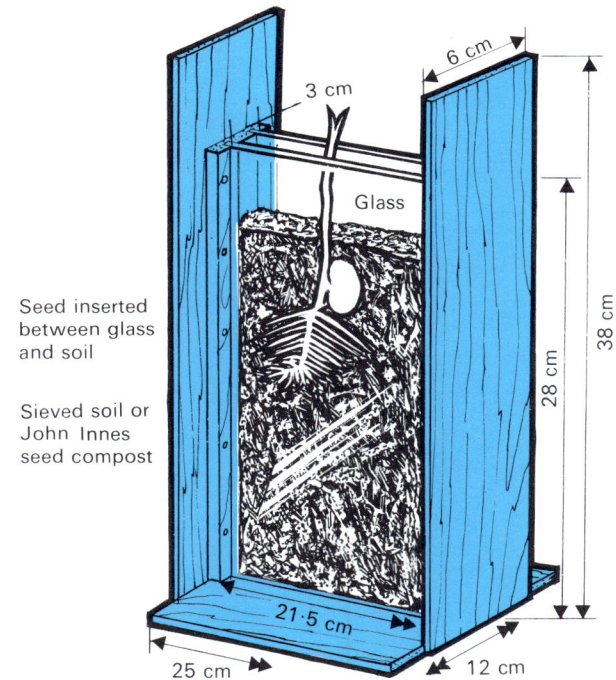

The most important comparisons to be made between these outdoor and indoor investigations will be those relating to the rate of development. Sufficient seeds should be sown out of doors to enable children to dig up specimens for examination.

During nature walks at this time, information about the size and rate of growth of wild seedlings could also be collected. Developing acorns and conkers can often be found among woodland litter and many seedlings flourish under hedgerows.

Recording
Children should be encouraged to use speech (and possibly a tape recorder), drawing and writing in describing exactly what they see and measure when their seeds germinate.

Checks for accuracy become increasingly appropriate the older children become.

A careful study of the children's records will soon reveal any lack of understanding. In the following work, for example, children at first used the word 'shoot' wrongly but soon corrected themselves in the light of further experience. No doubt discussion with the teacher helped here.

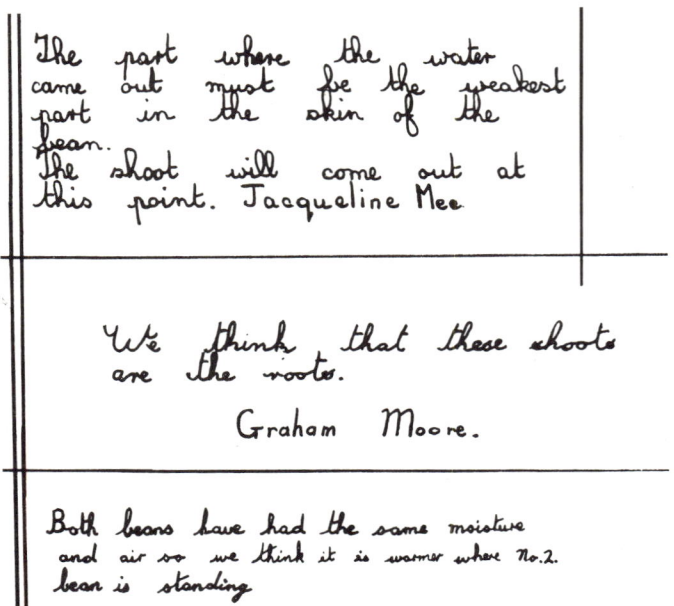

> The part where the water came out must be the weakest part in the skin of the bean.
> The shoot will come out at this point. Jacqueline Mee

> We think that these shoots are the roots.
> Graham Moore.

> Both beans have had the same moisture and air so we think it is warmer where No.2 bean is standing.

Dealing with questions
As this work progresses questions will soon arise. Here are examples.

What conditions help seeds to develop?
For trials use same numbers and same type of seed.

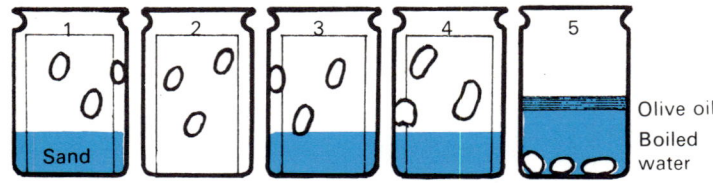

1. Give seeds air, water, warmth and light.

2. Deprive seeds of water.

3. Keep in a dark place.

4. Keep in a cold place.

5. Deprive seeds of air by covering them with water from which air has been expelled. The layer of oil prevents any further entry of air.

Do all fruits and seeds become plants?
For this investigation use seeds large enough to be handled easily. Place sets each of 100 seeds on trays of damp sand. Cover with pieces of polythene sheeting and keep at room temperature.

On which day did the largest number germinate?

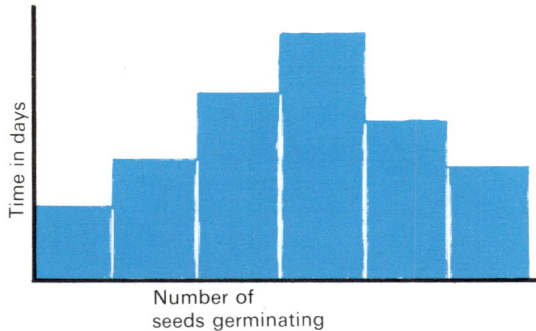

Keep any seeds that fail to germinate and test as above at three-monthly intervals.

It may be that some go through a longer period of inactivity before continuing their growth.

If the school has collections of seeds from previous years, stored in a dry state, some could be used for attempts to discover how far the length of storage affects the capacity to germinate.

Length of storage time in years	Percentage germination			
	Vetch	Sycamore	Acorns	Goatsbeard
1 year				
2 years				
3 years				

In this way the children can gain experience of dormancy. Reference can be made to the successful attempts to get the wheat seeds, found when the tombs of ancient Egyptians were opened, to germinate.

Why are shoots found growing out of tree stumps? A clue to the reason might be found by removing the terminal (top) buds on some twigs and then noticing any changes in buds at lower levels than those removed.

Can we make roots grow upward?
This is the time to introduce the idea of a germination sandwich.

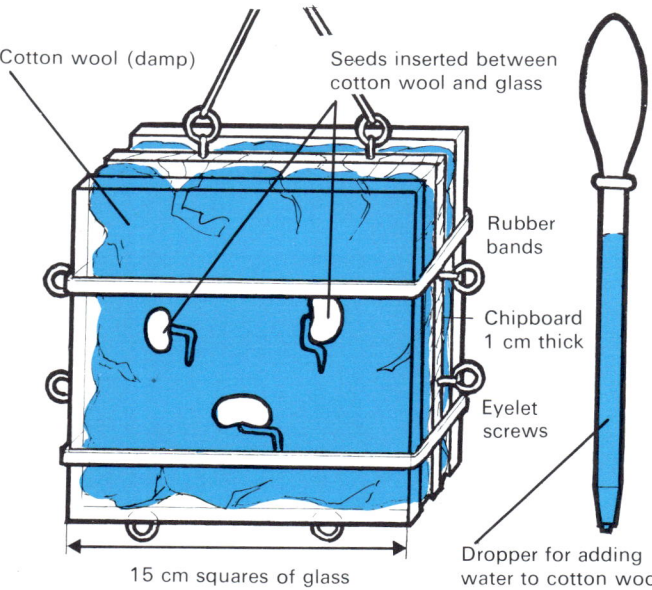

As the plants grow, this equipment can be turned and the effects of altering its position noted.

Can we have new plants without seeds?
1. Collect some willow twigs. Place them in water on return to school and regularly observe the lower ends. Plant some pieces in the garden when roots have formed.

2. Look out for a hedgerow containing blackberry bushes and then dig up the tip of a branch fixed to the ground and examine it carefully.

After this find a blackberry branch that can be bent over to bring its free end in contact with the ground. Fix it in this position with the help of metal meat skewers. Examine at regular intervals for the next two or three months.

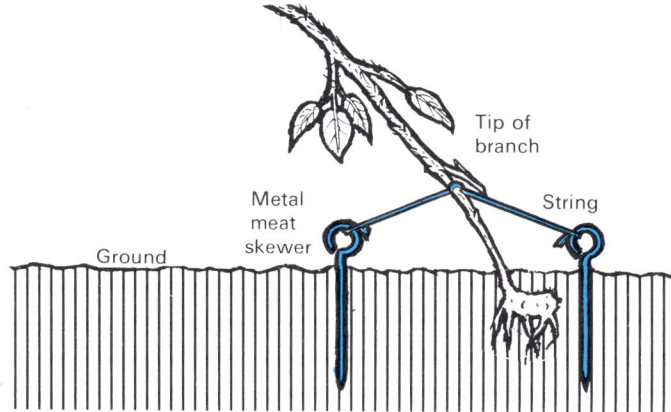

3. Collect some rhizomes, that is, horizontal underground stems, of:

Couch grass from a garden plot or allotment.
Water iris from the marshy border of a stream.
Wood sorrel from a hedgerow.

Cut these into 2-cm lengths and plant about 5 cm apart in moist John Innes seed compost in a propagating tray or seed box. Cover with polythene sheeting.

Which pieces give rise to new plants?

Treat a 'seed' potato in the same way. What must a piece contain to give rise to a new plant?

4. Dig up a fully grown plant of lesser celandine and carefully remove the bulbils (swellings) attached to its roots. Plant these singly in a seed box or in separate pots.

5. Collect single plants of creeping buttercup (*Ranunculus reptans*), wild strawberry (*Rosaceae fragilis*) or rock rose (*Potentilla tormentilla*). Make sure the root system is present. Plant these singly in the centres of cleared patches of soil each about 30 cm square, and observe regularly throughout the summer.

Beginning with eggs

These are often found unexpectedly during outdoor exploration or while digging and weeding garden plots. Some animals pass the winter in the egg stage, so good discoveries can be made in that season. In some cases identification may be impossible until the eggs hatch. Here is some information that may help children to discover the eggs of some creatures and to keep them in suitable conditions for observing the earliest stages of their development.

Type of find	Animal responsible	Places to search	Best times for searching	Conditions for hatching
Spawn	Frogs (batch) Toads (string) Newts (singly under leaves) Pond snails (strung on weed)	Ponds Ditches	April May	Place with weed in an aquarium or bowl of pond water. Tap water is also suitable after it has been stood for 24 hours to allow chlorine to escape. Keep cool and away from sunlight.
Singly or in batches	Butterflies Moths	On or under leaves	May or July	Place in a cardboard box with air holes in the lid. Keep dry. Add leaves of food plants when caterpillars begin to emerge, and transfer them on these to a rearing cage.
Singly or in batches	Land snails	Holes in moist earth	Summer	Place in suitable containers with some of the surrounding substrate. Label with place and date of discovery. Keep cool and do not allow surroundings to dry up. Observe each day.
	Slugs	Just below soil surface	Summer	
	Earwigs	Under bark. Holes	Early spring	
	Beetles	Under bark On plants In plant stems In soil In fungus caps and brackets	Various times	
Cocoons	Earthworms	Soil Under rotting leaves	Spring to autumn	
	Spiders	Cracks Under crossbars of fences	Autumn Winter	

Jam jar
Net
Screw-top jar
Rubber band
Air holes
Perspex lunch box

Type of find	Animal responsible	Places to search	Best times for searching	Conditions for hatching	
Concealed within other material	Frog-hoppers	In cuckoo spit on plants	July	Arrangement for living plant bearing cuckoospit or galls: Plastic bag, Bottle of water, Pot of soil	Arrangement for dry twig bearing a gall: Jam jar, Net, Dry sand
	Gall-wasps	In malformations on trees and leaves	Various times		
Miscellaneous	Unknown	Chance discoveries (Pond mud a good source)	Various times	Place in screw-top jars as above with some of the substrate in which found and wait for emergence. Pond mud should be placed in a jar with some pond water.	

On visits to seashores children should look out for the egg cases of whelks and dogfish and in spring the egg ribbons of sea slugs (Dorids) on rocky shores.

The actual emergence of a creature from its egg can provide an absorbing experience. For this reason, where conditions are suitable for setting up and maintaining an incubator, some fertile hen's eggs might be installed to enable children to see the emergence of the chicks at first hand.

If there is running water in the classroom or laboratory, developing trout eggs with their disappearing yolks will show children how much of the egg consists of a store of food to give the young a good start until they are strong enough to fend for themselves. (For further reference see the leaflet *A Trout Hatchery in School* referred to on page 45.)

If any of this material could be made available, other matters might be allowed to wait for a time so that children can be given time to appreciate this fully.

At this time it is also appropriate to remind children that all creatures do not hatch from eggs outside the parent's body. School pets and visits to farms may provide children with opportunities for becoming more familiar with the state of some animals very soon after their birth.

From early stages of development to maturity

During this time animals and plants may change in many ways, for example:

In size.
In the appearance of different parts.
In the form of the body, involving reorganisation of its materials.
In habits and behaviour.

In the same living things a number of these changes may go on simultaneously.

Measuring changes in size

Obviously the best way of finding out more about changes in size will be by measuring. Here are some methods that children might use.

Make a drawing of a growing plant exactly to size. This is an appropriate exercise for younger junior children.

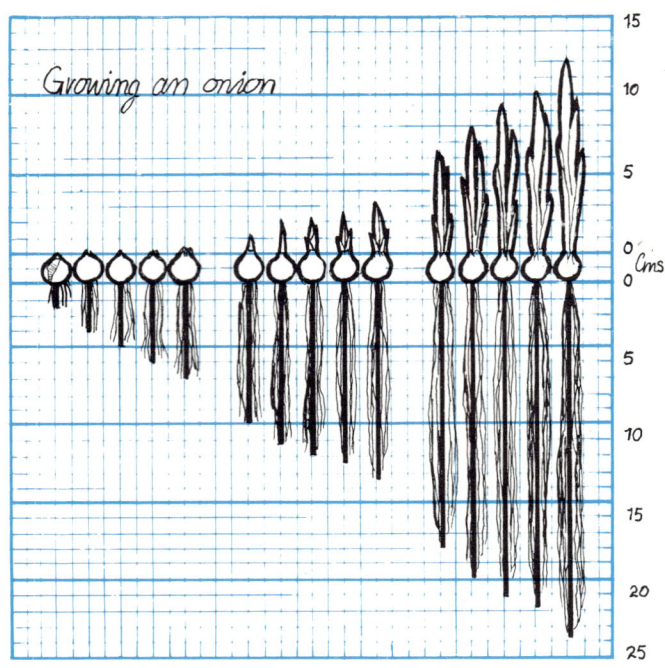

These children took regular measurements of the ten runner beans they grew by their classroom window and transferred their results on to a chart.

Different rates of growth

Do some parts of a plant grow more quickly than others? To find out use large seeds or fruits such as broad bean, acorn, sycamore or sunflower.

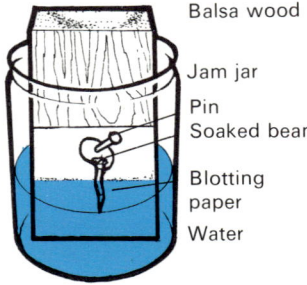

Balsa wood
Jam jar
Pin
Soaked bean
Blotting paper
Water

Set up an arrangement as shown in the diagram. Leave it at room temperature until the root is about 15 mm in length. Place cotton dipped in Indian ink against the root of the bean to make lines 2 mm apart. Allow growth to continue for another week or ten days. Measure distances between the lines. When the shoot has emerged and grown to a suitable length it can be treated in the same way.

Examining a series

Growth is often a slow process and some children may lose interest in their slowly changing specimens even though they may be dealing at the same time with other investigations. It might be more stimulating for them to collect and arrange specimens of plants and animals in a series, and then measure them.

Suitable material might be:

1. Sycamore seedlings from a woodland floor.

A series of sycamore seedlings.

2. Series of common weeds. The early stages of two weeds have been drawn below to aid recognition.

Groundsel

Shepherd's purse

3. Leaves on the same stem, such as those of privet, hawthorn, ivy.
4. Exoskeletons of crabs in all stages of growth which have been cast off through the summer and may be collected in large numbers on the banks of estuaries (eg at Dale Fort, Pembrokeshire) in late summer.
5. Shells of the common limpet (*Patella vulgata*).
6. Pond snails from the time of hatching in the aquarium.

Recognition of the early stages of weed seedlings may be obtained from *Identification of the Seedlings of Common Weeds*, Bulletin no. 179, Ministry of Agriculture and Fisheries (HMSO, 1959).
See also *Collins Pocket Guide to the Seashore*, page 132 (Collins, 1958), for distinguishing the common limpet from related species.

Measuring very small amounts

Some older children may like to construct equipment for this purpose.

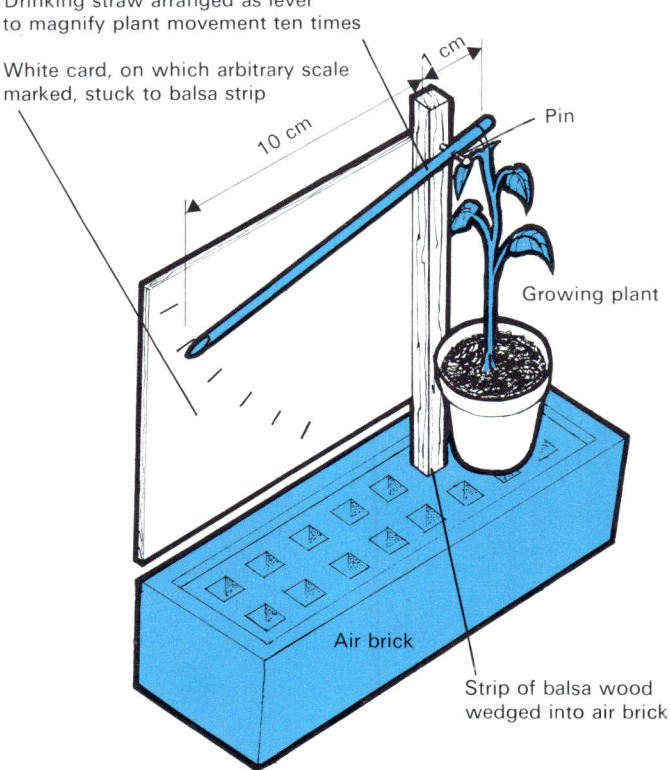

Drinking straw arranged as lever to magnify plant movement ten times

White card, on which arbitrary scale marked, stuck to balsa strip

1 cm

10 cm

Pin

Growing plant

Air brick

Strip of balsa wood wedged into air brick

Growing smaller

It is possible to collect measurements of creatures that grow smaller. Remove any planarians from a pond dipping catch, or attract some by placing some raw liver in a jam jar and suspending it by a string in the stagnant water of a ditch for a few hours.

Planarian

Place the creatures in separate small dishes containing some clean tap water that has been left standing for a few hours to allow chlorine to evaporate. (Do not use pond water as it contains natural food.) Measure the length and greatest width of each creature.

Give no food and take the same measurements daily.

Plot averages of results. What are these animals living on?

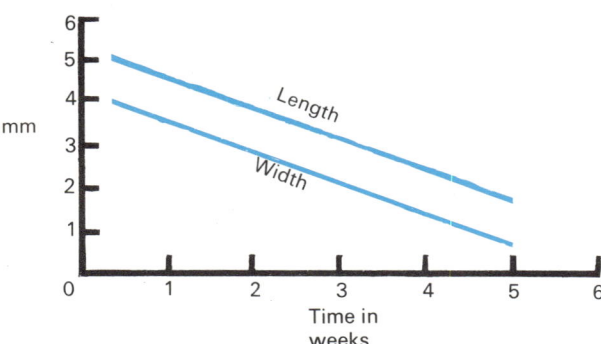

Return them to the pond after obtaining some results to allow recovery.

Spreading

Another long-term study for older juniors could be the spread of a plant over an area. Creeping buttercup, a small patch of daisies on the lawn, or two or three grass seeds sown in a cleared square metre of ground could be used for investigation.

Use a string grid (see Volume 4, page 53) for sub-dividing a square metre containing the plant.

Record weekly measurements of its growth reduced proportionally on squared paper. This is suitable for children who understand drawing to scale.

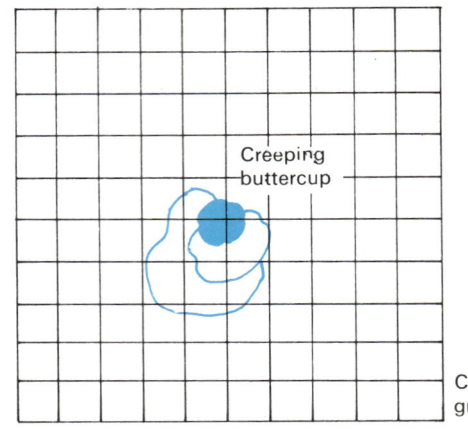
Creeping buttercup

Cm-squared graph paper

Measurements of mass

Weighing a guinea pig

A change in length may or may not be accompanied by a change in width, but this complication can be avoided by using measurements of increasing mass as evidence of growth.

Many young children weigh their pets regularly for this reason.

A way of weighing growing plants

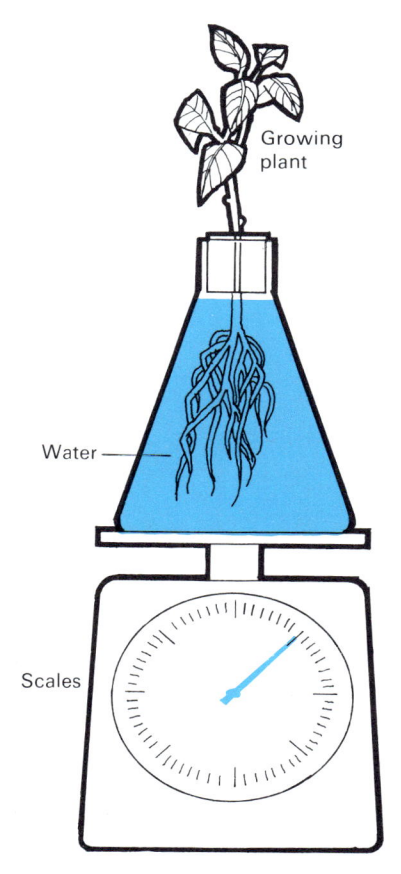

As water in the bottle is used by the plant, fresh supplies can be injected through the hole in the stopper by means of a syringe in order to keep the mass of the bottle + water constant.

Thus any increase must be due to plant growth.

The dry mass of a plant

This is the mass of material left after the removal of water. It is another useful measurement.

Leave the plant without water. Weigh it daily until two successive weighings give the same result. This is the dry mass of the plant.

This is a good way to compare plants of the same species at different stages of growth, for then it is not necessary to deal separately with different parts.

Grass mown from two similar areas of lawn given different treatments can also be measured after drying, by weighing.

Graphical records and patterns

Children should be encouraged to make similar series of measurements in different growing plants and record these results graphically. Then they may discover certain patterns occurring over and over again. Here are some examples.

1. A series of plants arranged in order of height.

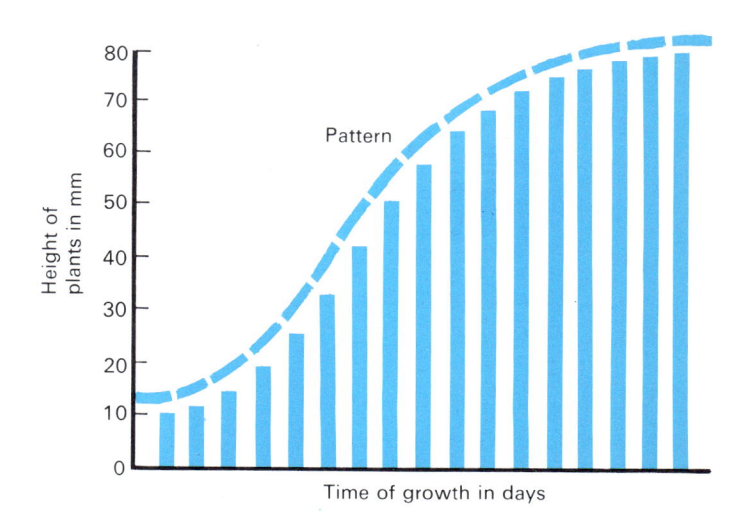

Here we have a fairly slow rate of growth at first followed by a steady increase in height and finally a levelling off of the measurements as the plants attain their maximum height.

2. The measurement of the length of leaves on a twig taken in order from base to apex.

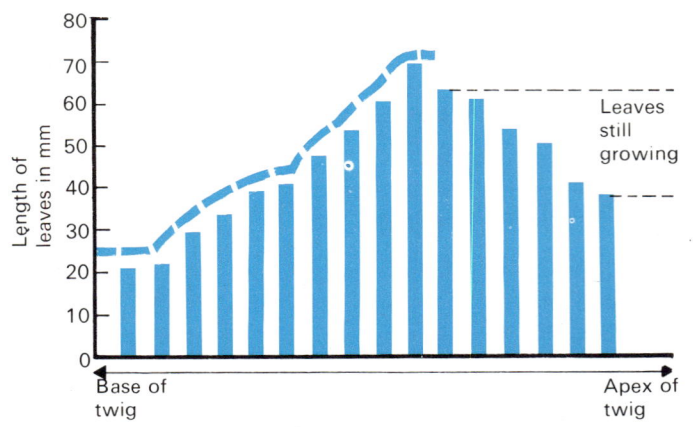

This is the pattern when the leaves are arranged in pairs. Leaves whose growth is complete form a steadily lengthening series, but beyond this the leaves still growing decrease in length the nearer they get to the apex of the twig. This pattern gives a method of finding the part of the twig where growth is still occurring.

3. The measurement of both the length and width of each leaf below the growing region of a twig, beginning at the base.

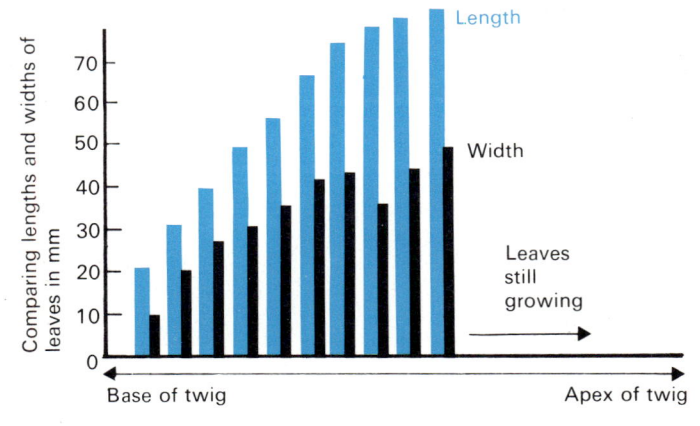

This shows another common characteristic of growth patterns: how different parts of the same thing grow to different extents. This differential growth gives the leaf its shape, in this case, longer than broad.

4. Recording the time of appearance of parts of different growing seedlings.

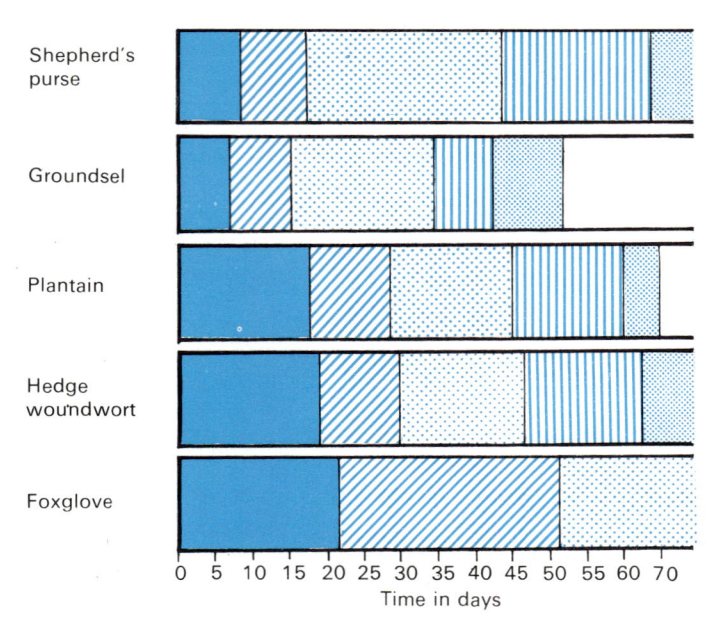

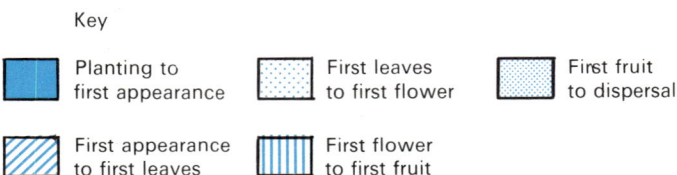

Key
- Planting to first appearance
- First appearance to first leaves
- First leaves to first flower
- First flower to first fruit
- First fruit to dispersal

The parts of different plants appear in the same order but there are great differences in the time this takes.

Would the timing be similar for plants of the same species?

Size at the adult stage
When children investigate changes in size they may gain enough experience to realise that living things eventually reach a size characteristic of their particular species. This is not a fixed size, it varies within a certain range. If they think of this in relation to the place where the plant grew or the creature lived they may suggest that the position within the range finally reached was influenced by environmental conditions that affected the organism while growing.

Interesting life histories

Some of the changes children get most satisfaction from following are those involved in the metamorphoses of butterflies, moths and frogs. Today there is a risk of many of these creatures disappearing from our countryside as the result of over-collecting, the use of poisonous sprays and the destruction of suitable habitats such as village ponds. Some members of county naturalists' trusts are trying to provide breeding grounds for butterflies and moths in some of their reserves by establishing food plants for the adults and their larvae. Children can actively contribute to the work of conservation by taking frogs they succeed in rearing to country ponds or ditches.

A list of butterflies and moths suitable for study by junior children is given in Volume 4 (pages 34–36) of *Using the Environment* together with details of food plants needed by their larvae and the months of the year when eggs can be found and adults may be expected to emerge from pupal cases.

The children should try to follow the *complete* life histories from egg to adult of any of these insects if they keep them in school. Full details for the maintenance of our commonest butterfly, the Cabbage White (*Pieris brassicae*), are also given in Volume 4 (pages 78–79). This animal, however, is a garden pest, so it should never be released indiscriminately. Ichneumon flies help to prevent its numbers from becoming excessive. The way in which they do so is another absorbing story (see Volume 3 Part 1, pages 27–28).

Although these life stories are so interesting, they are not easy for inexperienced children to record because changes in size, number of parts, form and habits so often take place all at the same time.

They need their teacher's help in organising their data. He or she might provide assistance by designing a chart, such as the one shown at the bottom of this page, with appropriate headings on which children could add details of their own observations.

If children use a chart like this they can still make their own discoveries, and obviously they cannot contribute to this record until they have done so. Older children (ten and eleven years) will often enjoy keeping diaries which give in their own words the life stories of their own specimens. One of the teacher's objectives here should be to help the children to produce records that gain steadily in depth and accuracy.

Even when children are deeply interested they can miss many things and enthusiasm may flag when a life cycle moves slowly. At these times a teacher ready to become a partner can provide incentives to renewed effort and progress. On the next page are some questions and suggestions for the teacher to use in such situations.

1969	The story of our frog tadpoles			
Date	What is it like?	What does it do?	Measurements	Drawings
1st March	Eggs black, round, evenly spaced in jelly	No movement, floating in the water	Eggs 2 mm across 4 cm jelly between each egg (approx.)	
4th March	Eggs getting longer	Slight wriggling movement	Eggs 4 mm in length, 2 mm in width	

The life story of the Cabbage White butterfly
Finding the eggs

In May keep a close watch in a garden on a cabbage patch or a border where nasturtiums are growing.

If you see Cabbage White butterflies fluttering about make careful notes of exactly what they do.

Try to make some estimations about their size. What other parts of the body are visible from a distance? Are there any differences in their wings?

If you notice any butterflies settling on plants watch very carefully. Do butterflies with a particular type of wing marking seem to settle more than others?

Later, search very carefully on the under surfaces of cabbage and nasturtium leaves to see if you can find any eggs. If you are successful collect the leaf and place its stem in water so that it remains alive. If you cannot find any eggs in the garden in May you may be more successful in August when there are many more butterflies about.

Why do you think the eggs are fixed to the under sides of leaves?

If your mother buys a cabbage from the greengrocer search very carefully between the outer leaves before she washes it. If you find any eggs place them carefully in a small plastic box with perforated lid and keep it in a cool dimly lit place. If the eggs hatch provide some pieces of cabbage for food while you make your first observations.

Observing the eggs

Place the piece of leaf with the egg cluster under the stereomagnifier or a large magnifier and watch carefully each day.

How many eggs are in the cluster? Is there always the same number of eggs in a batch? What can you discover about their shape, size and colour? Can you find any patterns?

If you know when the eggs were laid try to discover the length of time they take to hatch. You could find out:

The number of days before the first egg hatches.
The number of days before the last egg hatches.
The average time from laying to hatching.

Do all the eggs hatch?

Try to describe exactly what happened as an egg hatched. If you can collect any discarded egg cases try to discover whether they are waterproof.

Observing the caterpillar
If you cannot obtain any eggs of the Cabbage White butterfly, collect some cabbage caterpillars. How long is the smallest caterpillar you can find? How long is the largest caterpillar you can find?

If you cannot measure a caterpillar just after it hatches, search in books to try to find its length.

Spend as much time as you can watching your largest caterpillars under the stereomagnifier. Make a list of all the things you can see and add a description, such as:

The head—round and black,
    fixed to front end of body,
    5 mm across, 3 mm from front to back.

Are there any patterns on the body?

When you look at the animal very carefully indeed under the stereomagnifier you may see brown spots with darker rims on the sides of some segments. See whether you can discover breathing openings in the centres of these spots.

How many things on the body can you find to measure? Measure them regularly and see how many of them change in size. Keep records of the results of regularly weighing your caterpillars. Begin with the smallest stages you can find.

Observing the caterpillar moving
Do caterpillars spend most time moving or still? Do they remain close together or apart?

What can you discover about the ways they use their bodies and legs when they move? If you time the movements made by the parts of the body and legs with a stopwatch, do you find the actions taking place regularly or irregularly?

Do caterpillars move about more or less as they grow larger?

Can they move equally well:

Vertically and horizontally?
When upside down?
On different surfaces?

Can you discover any reason for your results?

Do they move much or little before, after, moulting? What are their movements like just before they turn into chrysalids?

35

Observing the caterpillar feeding
Spend some time carefully watching your caterpillars as they feed. How do they use their jaws and other parts of the body while doing this?

Can you time any of these movements or discover whether they are regular?

What part of the leaf do they eat?

Do they take pieces in any particular order?

What happens if you give a choice of food?

If you have caterpillars hatching from eggs try to discover when they begin feeding, and when matter first comes out from the other end of the body.

Do they feed without stopping or is there any time when feeding slows down?

Can you discover how much a caterpillar eats?

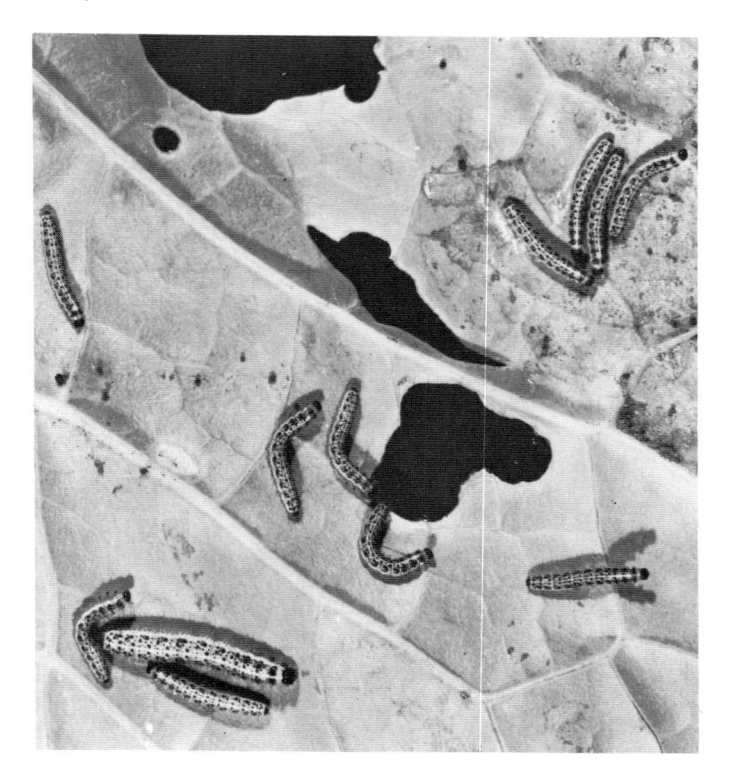

Observing the caterpillar moulting
If you can discover a caterpillar in the act of moulting, watch it very carefully. Where does the old body covering break? How does it cast this off? How long does this take? In what position is the caterpillar's body when moulting takes place?

When a caterpillar has moulted examine the cast-off material under a magnifier or microscope and describe what you see.

How does a caterpillar behave just before, just after, moulting? Is this different from its behaviour at other times?

Try to discover the number of times a caterpillar moults in its life.

Is the length of time between moults always the same?

Do caterpillars try to find any particular sort of place in which to moult?

Watching the caterpillar become a chrysalis
What is the caterpillar's length and width when full grown?

When it prepares to become a chrysalis how does it move? Where does it go? How does it remain in that position?

If you can discover a caterpillar becoming a chrysalis watch carefully and note all the changes that take place.

Collect some caterpillars ready to become chrysalids. Place them in separate small plastic boxes. Cover the boxes with Cellophane paper of different colours. What colour do the chrysalids in each box become? Are there any differences in the colours of the chrysalids?

How many things on the chrysalis can you find to measure?

How many things can you find that are like parts of adult butterflies?

Watching the butterfly
During the spring term observe chrysalids that have been kept throughout the winter at regular intervals to see if they make any movements.

If you notice any butterflies emerging from the chrysalid cases, watch very carefully and make a note of sequence of events. If possible time them with a stopwatch.

When the butterflies have recovered from their emergence transfer them to an outdoor cage and observe them carefully at regular intervals. A photograph of such a cage in which food plants for the butterfly can grow naturally, has been included in Volume 4, page 36.

Observe these creatures carefully at regular intervals. To what plants are they attracted?

37

Make a list of different parts of the body and describe them carefully. If possible use a stereomagnifier to look at any butterflies that die.

Measure the size of different parts.

Describe the differences in the black markings on the wings. Consult a reference book to see which markings indicate males and which females.

With a dropper place small drops of honey on leaves and flowers in the outdoor cage and watch butterflies feeding.

Use a needle to unroll a butterfly's tongue. The illustration shows how the creatures should be held for this purpose.

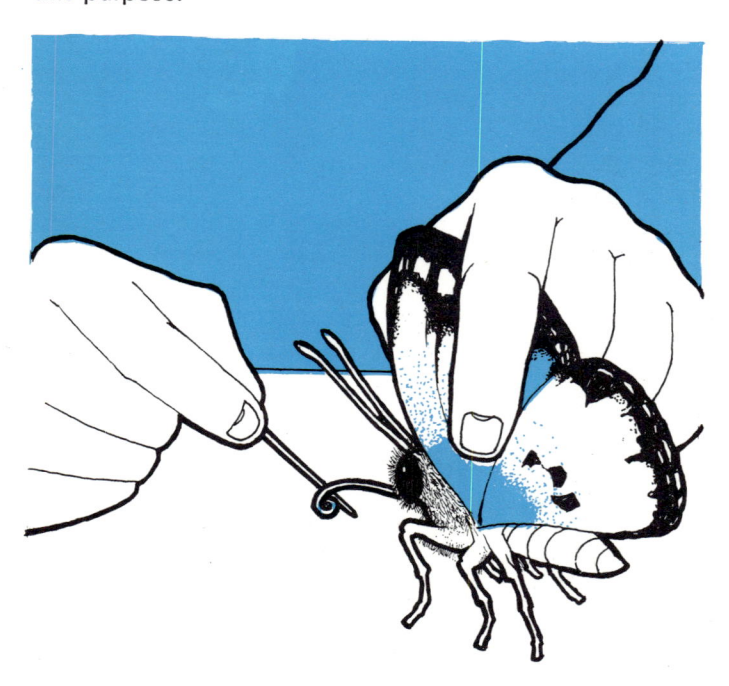

Do butterflies go more frequently to plant material of certain colours if no honey is on them?

If you see two butterflies coming together, and one is male and the other female, see whether the male tries to fertilise the female. Watch carefully and try to see whether any eggs are laid.

Things to discover about frog tadpoles in a classroom aquarium

What shape and size and colour are the actual eggs? By what approximate distance are they separated by jelly?

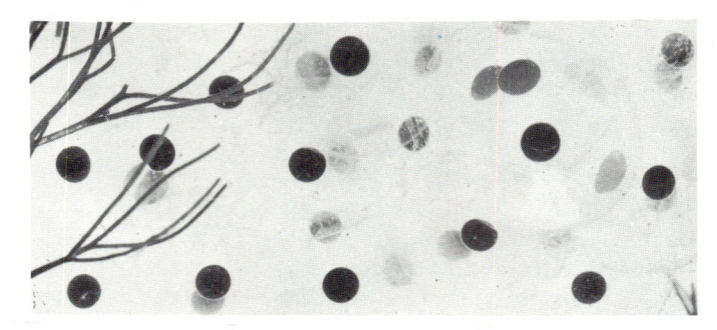

How do the eggs change with regard to shape and size? Include dates in this part of the record.

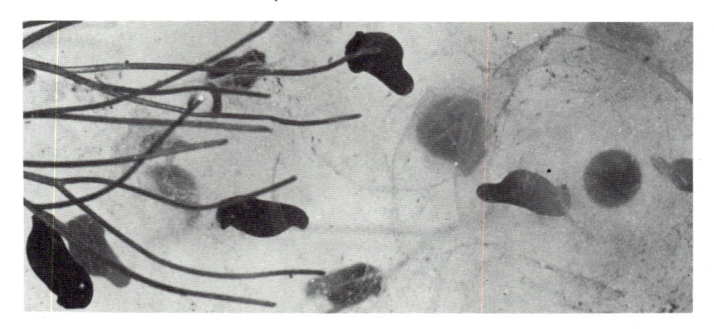

Is it possible to describe any movements made by tadpoles as they try to leave the surrounding jelly?

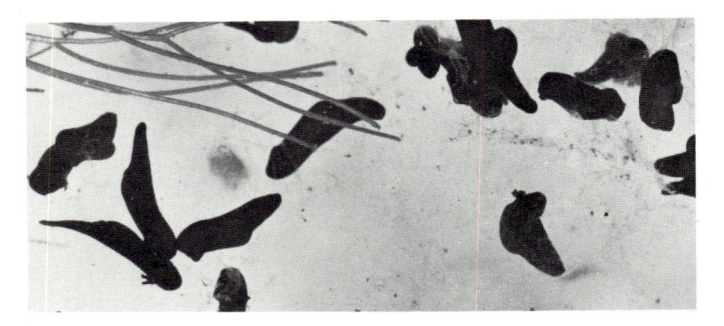

Does the egg's position in the mass of spawn affect the time when the tadpole tries to wriggle out of the mass, or do they all emerge together?

Try to make some drawings of tadpoles that have just emerged from the jelly. What size are different parts of the body at this stage?

How do the newly emerged tadpoles spend their first day after leaving the jelly? What proportion of this time is given to moving and feeding?

When they move do they move quickly or slowly?

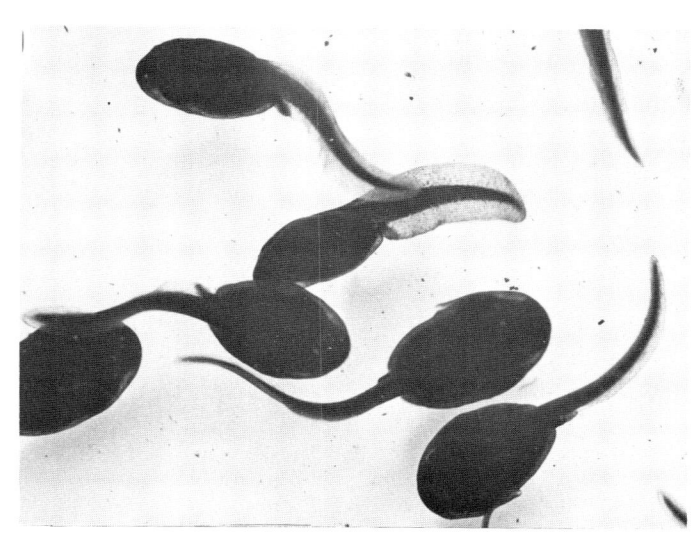

How soon after leaving the jelly do the feathery gills of tadpoles become visible; the creatures begin to swim actively?

What do the creatures use at this stage as a means of propulsion?
Can you estimate their speed of movement?

Note: one drop of chloroform in water in a small petri dish will slow down movement and enable creatures to be seen more easily under the magnifier.

What are they now using for food?

Make a note of the date of sighting the first trace of hind limb buds.
Can you describe the changes that then take place in these hind limbs?
Try to include approximate measurements and dates.
Make a note of the date when you find that the external gills have completely disappeared.
What is the approximate length of a tadpole at this stage?
Try to make a dated record of increases in size from the time of disappearance of the external gills. Your observations might include information about the length and width of the trunk and length of the tail.
Does this size relationship between trunk and tail change as development continues?
Whereabouts in the tank do the tadpoles spend most of the school day at this stage?
In what position are the hind limbs now when the creature moves rapidly?

39

How does the development of forelimbs beneath the skin affect the size of the trunk?

Do both front limbs appear at the same time? Give the date when this happens.

How long is this after the hind limbs are fully developed?

What changes in shape to the mouth are noticeable at the time that the forelimbs become visible?

On what date were the tadpoles' early attempts to breathe air at the water surface obvious?

Offer a small piece of raw meat, some water fleas. Are the tadpoles ready to feed on this material? Or in other words, are they becoming carnivorous?

Note: if raw meat is used, suspend it from a piece of cotton and remove it from the tank after one hour.

How do the colour and body and tail lengths change after the appearance of the forelimbs? Again include dates in your record. On what date:

1. Does the head appear as distinct from the trunk?
2. Do the eyes become larger and protruding?

How do these animals behave now when a few rocks are placed in the aquarium?

Changes in adult plants and animals

When living things are able to multiply, we say that they are mature, but changes can still happen, and these often relate to increases in number.

The following material might be investigated.

1. Duckweed
Place a few plants in dishes of pond water. Count the number of leaves.

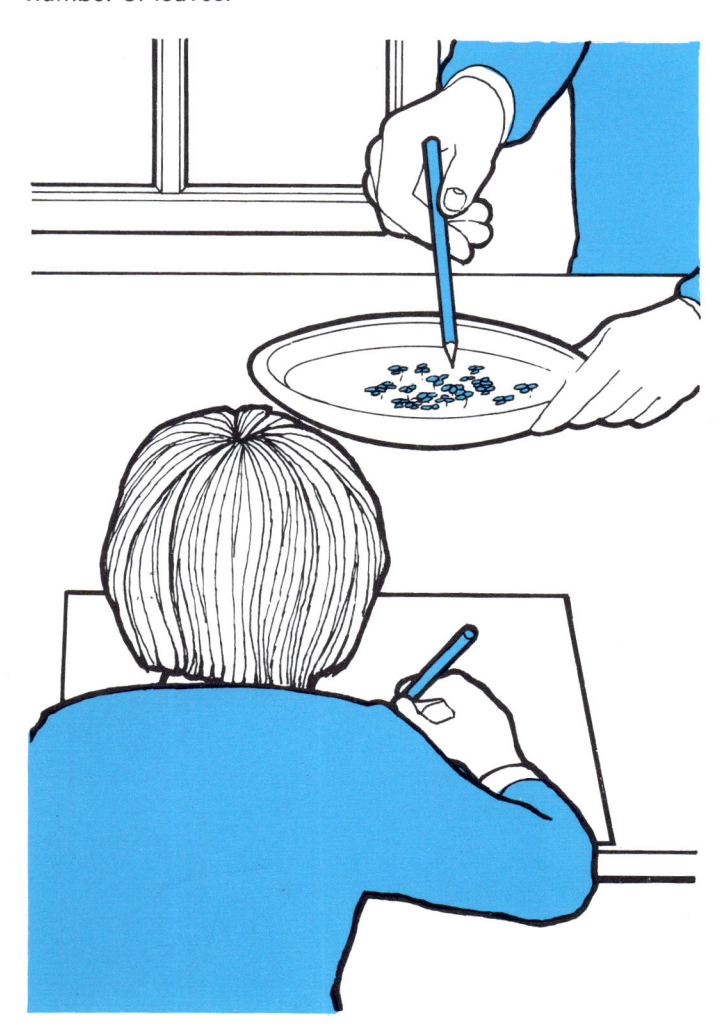

Keep in good conditions, with warmth and sunshine.

Top up the water when necessary.

Count the leaves each week.

2. Daphnia (water fleas)
In summer, pond water containing these animals can be obtained easily.

Transfer a few to a small tank of filtered pond water.

At weekly intervals supply with food consisting of a little thick paste made by mixing some malted milk powder (Horlicks) with some rotten egg.

Observe the culture carefully to see whether the population is increasing. When it looks as if it is, remove a little water from the tank.

Use a syringe to transfer 10 ml of this water into a small transparent dish. Stand this on a dark background and count the number of daphnia it contains. Continue examining in this way water extracted from the tank at five-day intervals.

Show the results of the count by means of a graph.

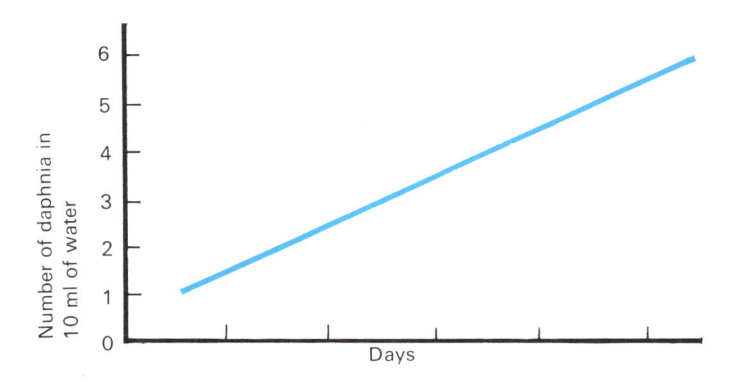

What might happen if the numbers in the tank continue to increase at this rate?

This investigation could also be used to discuss the technique of sampling, if the work is being done by older children who are ready for this mathematical idea.

Seasonal changes—studying deciduous trees

These studies can be a most effective means of providing children of about eleven years of age with experience of the influence of different weather conditions. Pairs or single children could adopt for a year deciduous trees around the school, and their observations and comparisons could form illustrated books, which they could then bind and present to the school library.

Obviously each child will also tackle numerous shorter studies while developing this long-term work.

Here are some suggestions and leading questions.

The winter stage

At this time of the year the following observations might be made:

The general shape and height of the tree.
The way in which its branches arise from the main stem.
The height at which branches leave the main stem.
The direction in which the branches point.

The colour of the bark.
Patterns formed by markings and grooves on the bark.
Interesting patterns on the underside of bark stripped from a dead branch, for example, burrows made by the elm bark beetle.

Markings on twigs such as leaf and girdle scars and lenticels. What causes such markings?

Note: for regular observations twigs left on the branch should be marked with metal rings or with coloured tape. This will enable children to make measurements at regular intervals of the length of buds, their colour, size, position on the stem and length of the internodes, and thus to discover the extent to which these things change.

The spring stage

Do leaf or flower buds develop first? Observe some twigs kept in water and make a careful record of what happens.

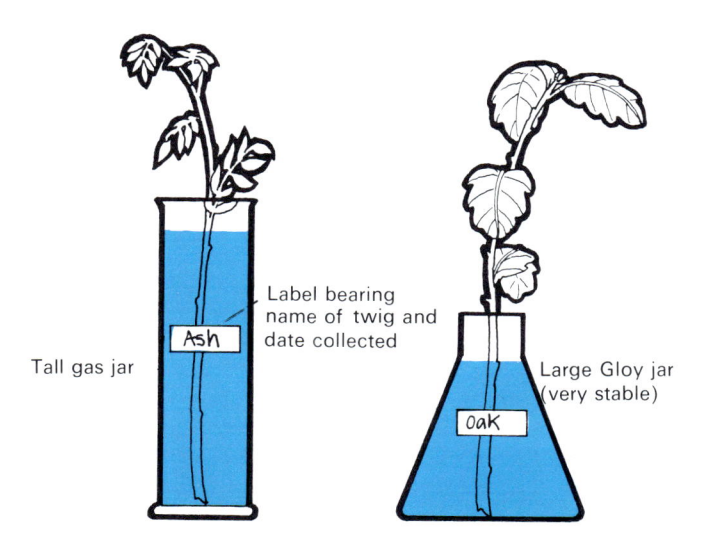

Tall gas jar — Ash
Label bearing name of twig and date collected
Large Gloy jar (very stable) — Oak

Children should use separate jars for each of their **twigs**. Before placing them in water, lengths of about 5 mm should be cut from the lower ends. This should remove any airlocks that may be blocking the open ends of the tubes, which take up water (xylem tubes).

Avoid giving twigs too much heat or sunlight, for this may cause the delicate small leaves to dry rapidly.

Changes while the buds on twigs open are far from easy for children to record. The teacher might suggest that each child looks very carefully at his or her twig on alternate days at the same time of day and makes a large drawing of its end (terminal) bud.

The efforts of different children could then be fixed to a group chart designed for the purpose. In these days when many children have their own Instamatic cameras some may even like to try photography as a method of recording.

Our opening buds		
Twigs	15 March	17 March
Horse-chestnut	Length 2.3 cm	Length 2.6 cm
Hawthorn		

Other children could make similar records of collections of twigs kept in different environmental conditions.

When are the bracts of the buds shed?
Can you collect evidence of the way the flowers are pollinated?
What parts of the flowers are shed? What remains?
Is there any relationship between the areas of different leaves on a twig and the position they occupy?
When are the first signs of fruit visible?

The summer stage

What can you discover about:

The increase in mass of fruits? Samples of ten should be weighed at regular intervals.
The number of fruits produced? How could this be estimated?

Note the date of the first sign of fruit dispersal. Do the fruits bear attachments? What can you do to discover their uses? (See Volume 3 Part 1, pages 52–55.) How is the fruit protected? What does it contain? You may discover this more easily if you soak the fruit first to make it soft.

Does anything cause damage to the tree?

Look at the trunk and lower branches for holes, outgrowths, and signs of gnawing.
Look at leaves and fruits. Collect a number of samples (ten per sample), look for marks and holes, and record percentage affected each time.

The autumn stage

Are the fruits shed rapidly or retained through the autumn?

By what date do no fruits remain on the tree?

In what ways do the leaves change? Look at the colour sequence, the size, shrivelling, etc.

When do the first leaves fall? By what date is the tree bare?

Study and measure the bare twigs you marked last winter and compare your new observations with those made then. Where has growth occurred?

If possible examine cross-sections of the trunk or branch of similar trees. What do the growth rings suggest?

For further information about studying trees see *Trees*, Science 5/13 (Macdonald Educational, 1973).

Other useful material

So far we have dealt with small things, some of which could be reared and observed without too much difficulty in any school. Where schools have generous accommodation and facilities and a member of staff or parent with special expertise is available, a much wider range of work will be possible. Perhaps the development of some of the following living things could then be studied.

References

For honey bees: *Science Teaching Techniques, no. 7, Bee-keeping in the Secondary School,* by J. Ryding (John Murray, 1959).

For trout: *A Trout Hatchery in School,* School Natural Science Society Leaflet no. 5, by E. M. Tuke.

For fish: *Animals in Schools,* Universities Federation of Animal Welfare, by J. P. Volrath, 1955: *Keeping Animals in Schools,* Department of Education and Science (HMSO, 1959).

Organism	Changes	Necessary facilities	Expertise in an adult
Honey bees	Complete life history: egg ↓ imago	Observation hive	Knowledge of bee-keeping
Locusts		Suitable cage maintained at temperature of 34°C day, 28°C night	Interest Not difficult
Trout eggs	Growth and development of embryo from egg to adult	Space Source of running water, sink, Marley guttering or plastic trays to serve as containers	Interest Not very difficult
Sticklebacks	Breeding behaviour	Space and large aquarium	Aquarist knowledge
Tropical fish	Breeding and growth	Tropical aquarium	
Goldfish	Breeding and growth	Biology pool	
Budgerigars	Egg-laying, hatching, growth	Space and cage away from quiet areas	Interest Not difficult
Chicks	Incubation, hatching, growth	Space and incubator	Knowledge of animal husbandry
Small mammals: Rabbits Guinea pigs Gerbils Rats Mice	Growth and development (do not handle too soon or parent may eat young)	Space Suitable cages Food supply (Stock from an accredited dealer)	

For budgerigars: *Animals in Schools,* UFAW, by J. P. Volrath; *Science Teaching Techniques, no. 9, The Budgerigar as a Focus of Interest for Scientific Studies,* by Sister Marie Josephine, SND (John Murray, 1962).

For snails and slugs: School Natural Science Society Leaflet no. 45, by E. M. Tuke.

For invertebrates, pond life, amphibia, reptiles, farm animals, poultry: *Keeping Animals in Schools.*

For chicks, small mammals: *Animals in Schools; Keeping Animals in Schools.*

For newts: *Science Teaching Techniques, no. 4, Keeping Newts in Captivity,* by A. Leutscher (John Murray, 1955).

General: *Animals in the Home and Classroom,* by T. J. Jennings (Pergamon, 1971).

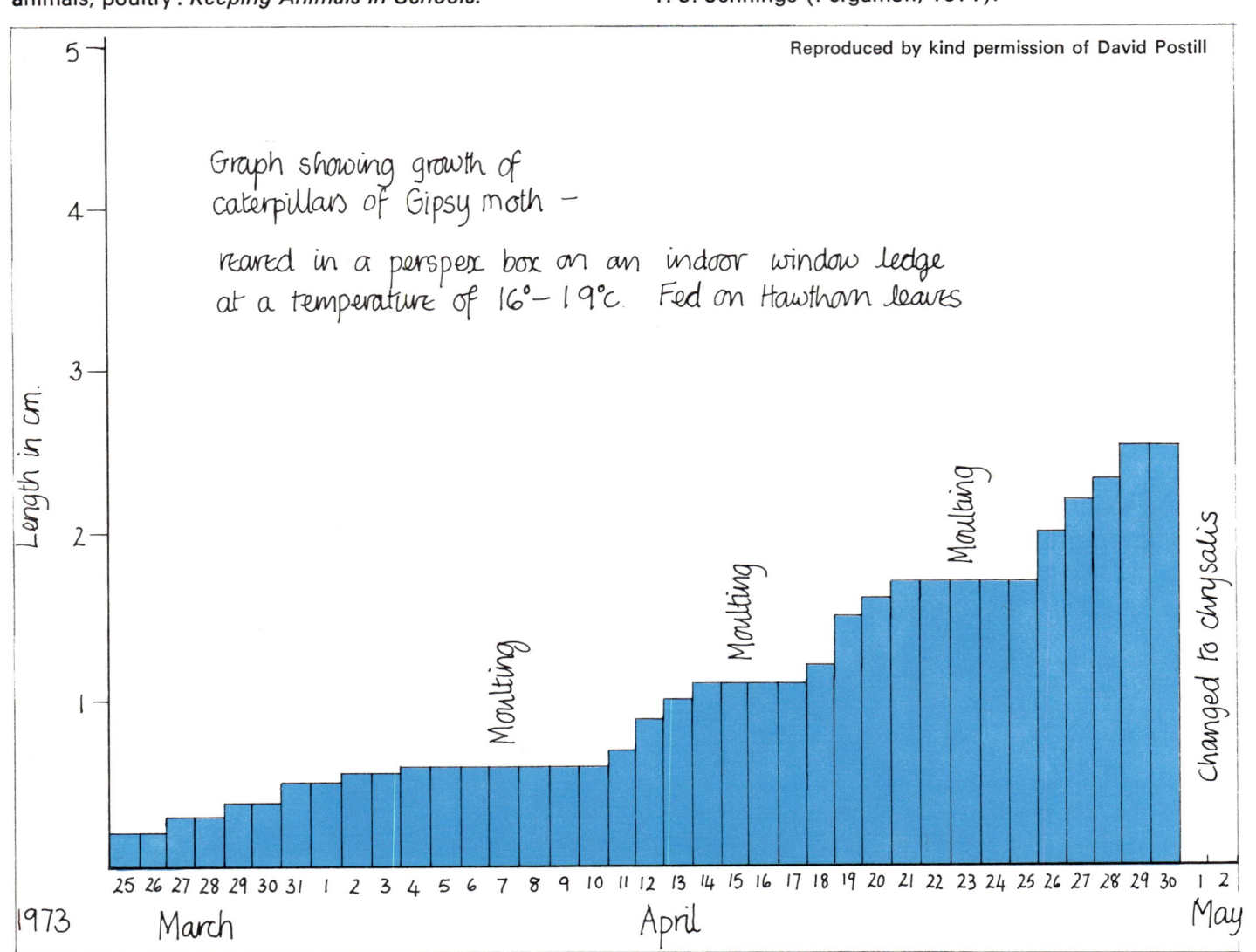

Reproduced by kind permission of David Postill

Graph showing growth of caterpillars of Gipsy moth — reared in a perspex box on an indoor window ledge at a temperature of 16°–19°C. Fed on Hawthorn leaves

3 The changing landscape

Many changes in landscape have taken place so slowly that they can only be traced from evidence in the rocks. In order to appreciate the great periods of time involved, children must develop the ability to think in terms like a 'thousand million years', something very different from the hours or days between changes during unsettled weather or the varying numbers of days, weeks or few years living things need for completing their growth and development.

When children begin to consider landscape, they are approaching a vast field of inquiry, for there are many ways in which changes affecting it can be followed, for example:

Horizontally, over the surface.
Down through the soil and rocks.
Backward to past eras.
Onward through the changing seasons.

Observing the land's surface

Children thoroughly enjoy outdoor expeditions and journeys, especially when their opportunities of making discoveries are not destroyed by a preliminary talk about 'what they will find'. On the other hand the teacher still has the problem of making sure that significant features of the landscape are not missed.

The chance to encourage careful observation comes when a good viewpoint is reached such as the summit of Leith Hill in Surrey with the fields and villages like a great patchwork below, or the first view eastward from the top of the Wallace Monument at Stirling, whence the River Forth can be followed as it winds in great meanders towards Edinburgh.

These are good moments for landscape sketching. The technique can be taught and the equipment prepared before the expedition begins.

The main problem in producing a quick drawing of the essential features in a landscape is that of proportion; so often the edges of the paper are reached when the sketch is half complete. An old picture frame helps here.

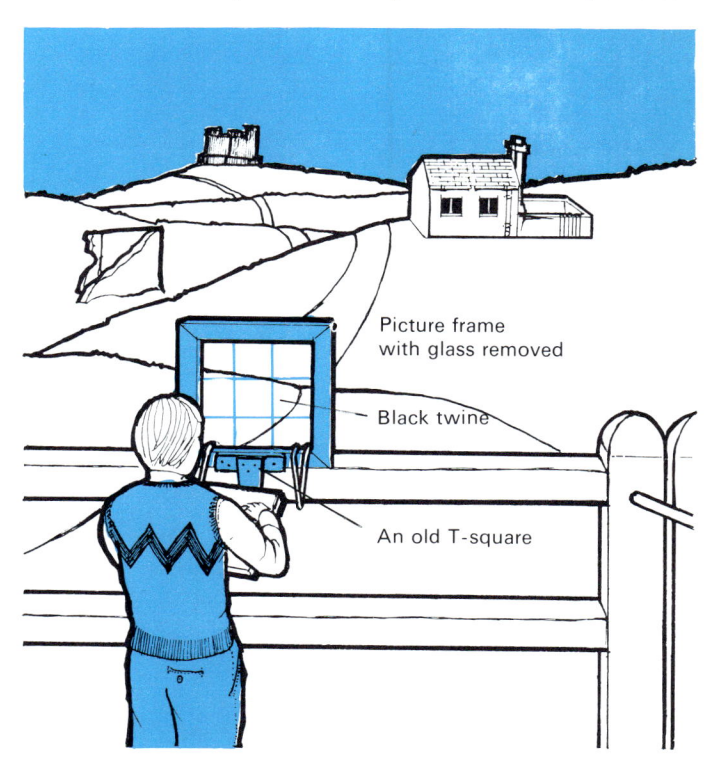

The apparatus shown here can be mounted on a pole, tied to a gate, or held by a child for the artist to sketch the enclosed view.

The main shapes and landmarks can then be drawn on paper marked to correspond to the smaller spaces within the frame.

While children work and the teacher circulates, there will be opportunities for questions and discussion. Comparison of sketches made from various viewpoints or by artists facing in different directions will soon reveal changes and contrasts. On return to school, children can relate their sketches to a map of the same area and so give its symbols concrete meaning.

In the guide *Starting with Rocks* (page 18) (which is part of the Schools Council Development Project on Environmental Studies published by Rupert Hart-Davis, 1973) another method of producing sketches of the countryside is described. This involves the children in adding their own observations, captions and symbols to diagrams which their teacher has prepared beforehand with the aid of colour transparencies.

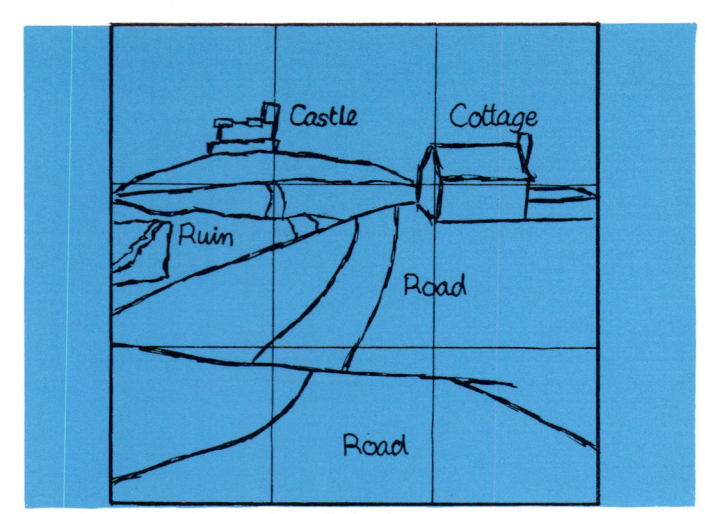

Landscape sketch seen through the frame

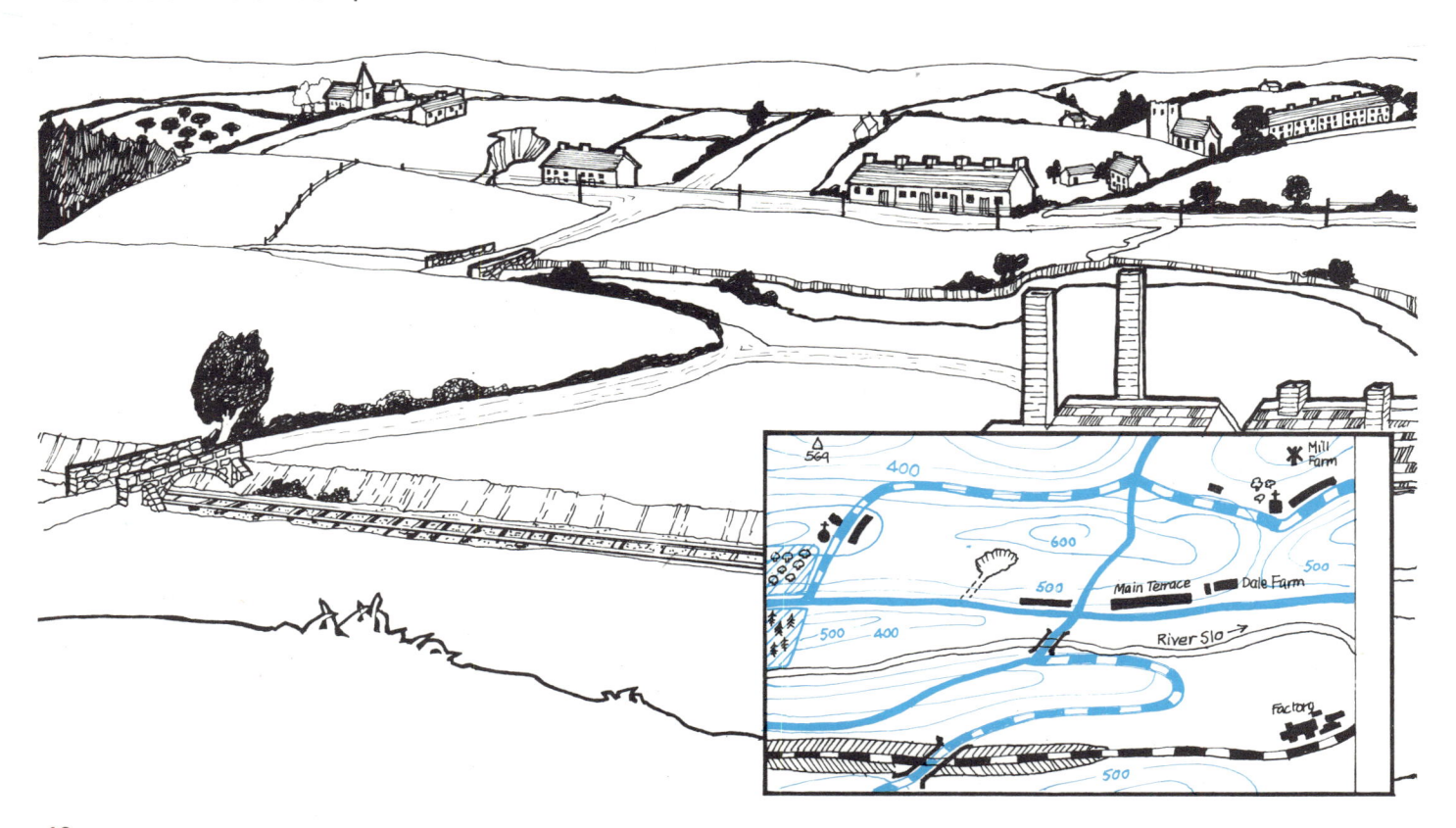

A local activity

As with earlier 'I spy' work, the children's powers of observation can be used to good effect as they come and go in their own time.

Do people use the land around our school in different ways?

This question can be the start of a class investigation in which differently coloured map pins can be used to make a key to represent children's discoveries about what people do with land. They will need a large blank base map of the district which can be made by the teacher with the help of an Ordnance Survey map. On this they can record observations made at any time during a month.

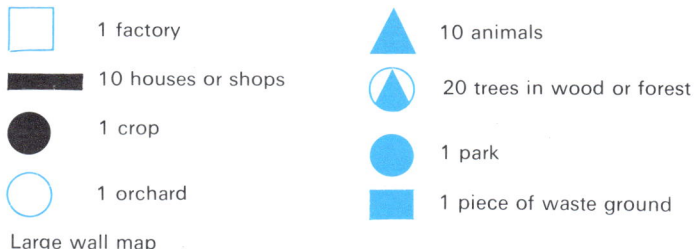

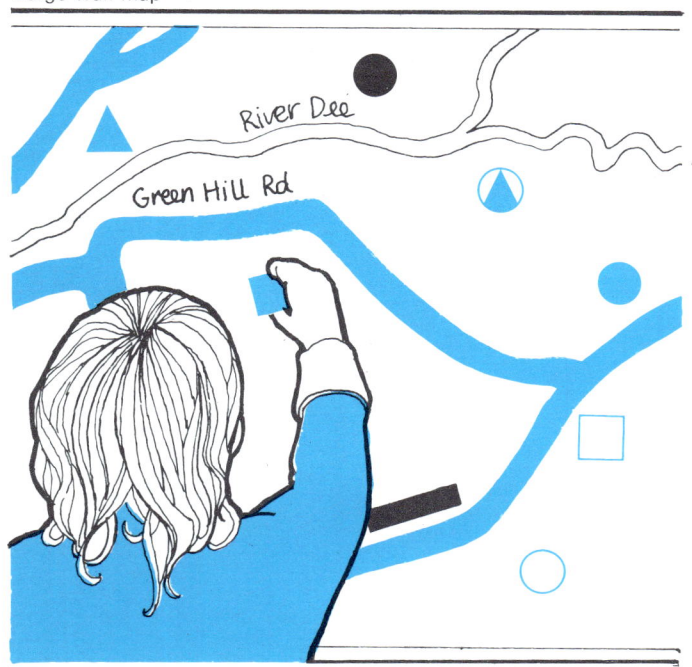

- ☐ 1 factory
- ▬ 10 houses or shops
- ● 1 crop
- ○ 1 orchard
- ▲ 10 animals
- ◓ 20 trees in wood or forest
- ● 1 park
- ■ 1 piece of waste ground

Large wall map

Looking downwards into the soil

Most young children find great satisfaction in digging and grubbing about in sand or garden soil. When they get a little bit older they will often stand and watch soil being moved on a huge scale as great mechanical diggers rapidly carve motorways and tunnels through deposits and hillsides formed from the erosion and deposition of millions of years.

These machines often leave soil sections exposed. This enables children to study vertical changes in the land and record them in an interesting way.

Soil monoliths

These are scale models of exposed profiles, as soil sections are usually called.

Measure the depth of the different layers of soil exposed. Collect a sample of soil from each layer and label it according to its position in the profile.

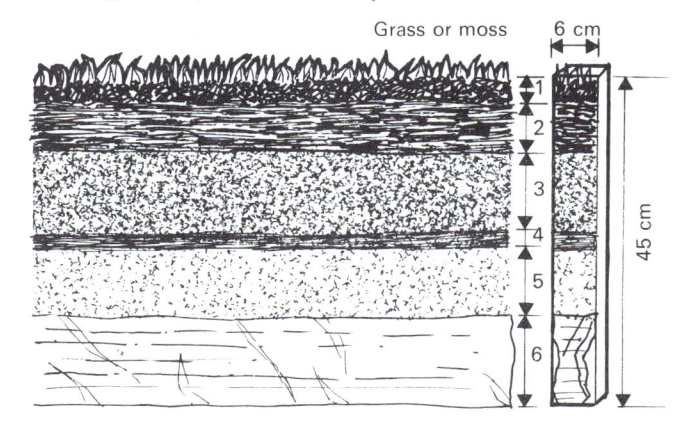

On a strip of wood draw lines to mark off areas corresponding in proportion to the actual layers of soil in the profile. Coat the surface of the wood with a thick layer of liquid glue (Casco or Bostik). Scatter appropriate soils from the samples taken over each marked part. Leave in a horizontal position until the glue sets.

When the children put a number of these monoliths side by side, the differences between soils from various places become very obvious.

Looking backwards in time

For these investigations children need things from the past to compare with their own observations.

Armed with a portable tape recorder, they will set off happily to try to tap the reminiscences of elderly people. They can be encouraged to turn to old maps, prints, and local archaeological discoveries for evidence of the ways in which people have used the same land in the past. Sooner or later they will see fossils in a local museum, or find them themselves. When they try to relate these to living organisms, they can go on to further comparisons between patterns, size and numbers of parts.

Are trilobites anything like woodlice?

A trilobite

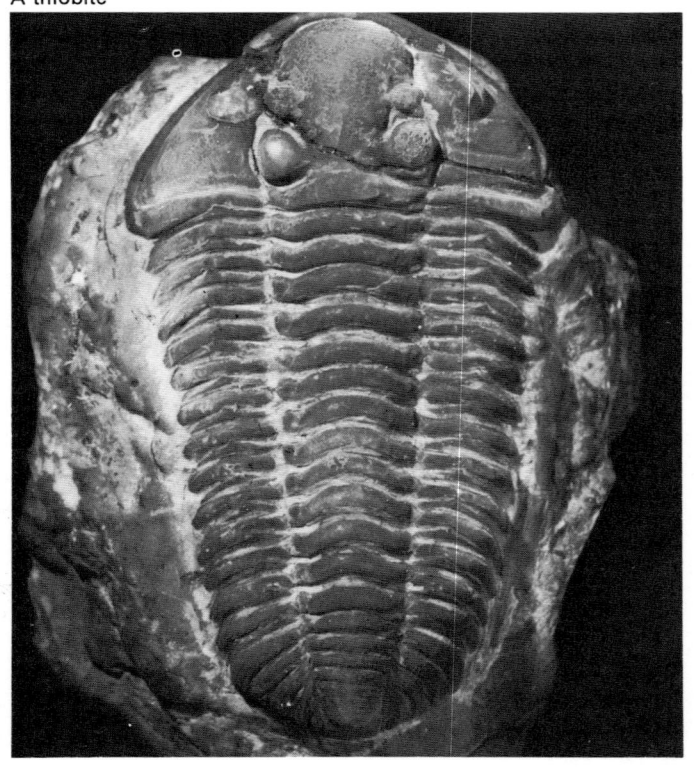

Calamites and Lepidodendron are fossils of some of the great tree-like plants of ancient forests that became coal.

What small plants remind us of them today? (Field horsetail, *Equisetum arvense,* and club mosses of moorlands and heaths.)

An ancient coal forest

What could we look at to help us to visualise some of the insects and amphibia that inhabited the coal forests? (Dragonflies and newts.)

Fossil of a mollusc with a shell in one piece (a univalve)

The beach can provide bivalve and univalve shells with many similarities to fossil molluscs. Comparisons with these fossils will demonstrate to children the extreme slowness of change among these forms of life.

Shells from the beach can also be used for activities that help children to realise what some fossils really are and how they have been formed.

Prepare a square of Plasticine 80 mm × 80 mm and 10 mm in thickness. Press a small cockle shell into this. Impressions like this made millions and millions of years ago in mud have been preserved after the shell has disintegrated and mud surrounding it has hardened into rocks of gault clay.

Now mix up some plaster of Paris with water and use this to fill such an impression. When this has set, remove the Plasticine and we now have a cast of the shell. Through the ages spaces left by the disintegration of shells have become filled with mud which has hardened into rock and which gives fossils in the form of casts and these too are often found in gault clay.

Fossil sea urchin

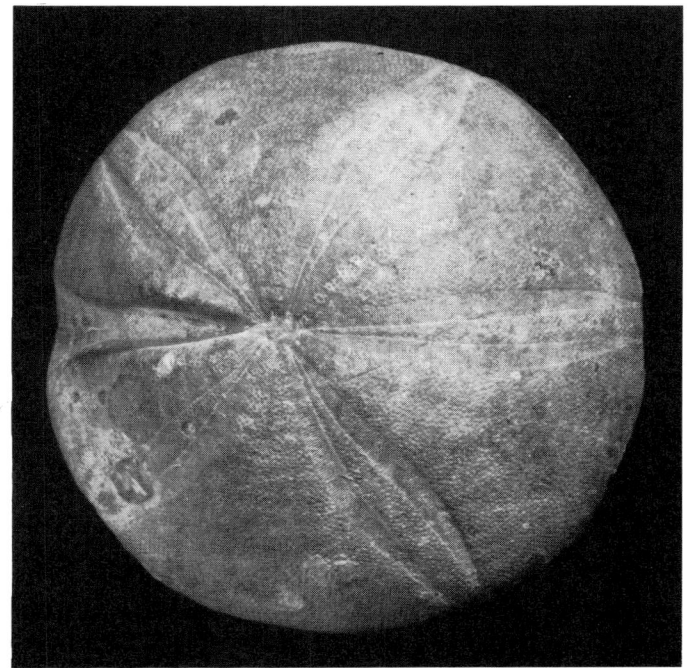

A dried shell of a sea urchin (above) might be found in a sea-side junk shop and this could be used for comparison with fossil sea urchins in the form of casts.

Specimens of ammonites (below) and belemites, or the great casts and models of dinosaurs in the British Museum of Natural History, will provide ways of introducing the idea of extinction and will also provide a good opportunity for warning against over-collecting.

When were these things alive?
Did they all live at the same time?

These questions will soon be posed by the children, and then it is time to help them to begin to develop some conception of geological time.

The geological time scale

Children should start by trying to grasp the idea of a million, and for this they will need to see a million things. Here graph paper can prove useful. A piece of graph paper 10 × 20 cm will give 5000 2-mm squares. If children lay 200 such pieces side by side on the hall floor, or stick them end to end, they can see 1 million small squares.

How many children would have to drop 1000 lentils or grains of rice into jam jars to collect a million? Is there a good method of estimating a million grains of sand?

Then children could be asked to think about the time span between two Christmases or two birthdays, and imagine this happening a million times. It would be appropriate at this juncture to introduce a large diagram of the geological time scale, so that they can see what a tiny part of it the time they have just imagined occupies.

If children let 1 cm represent 1 million years, they can transfer the geological time scale on to 6 metres of cotton tape. But they will need another 10 metres if they wish to include the Pre-Cambrian rocks, which took about 1000 million years to form and came before anything shown on this scale.

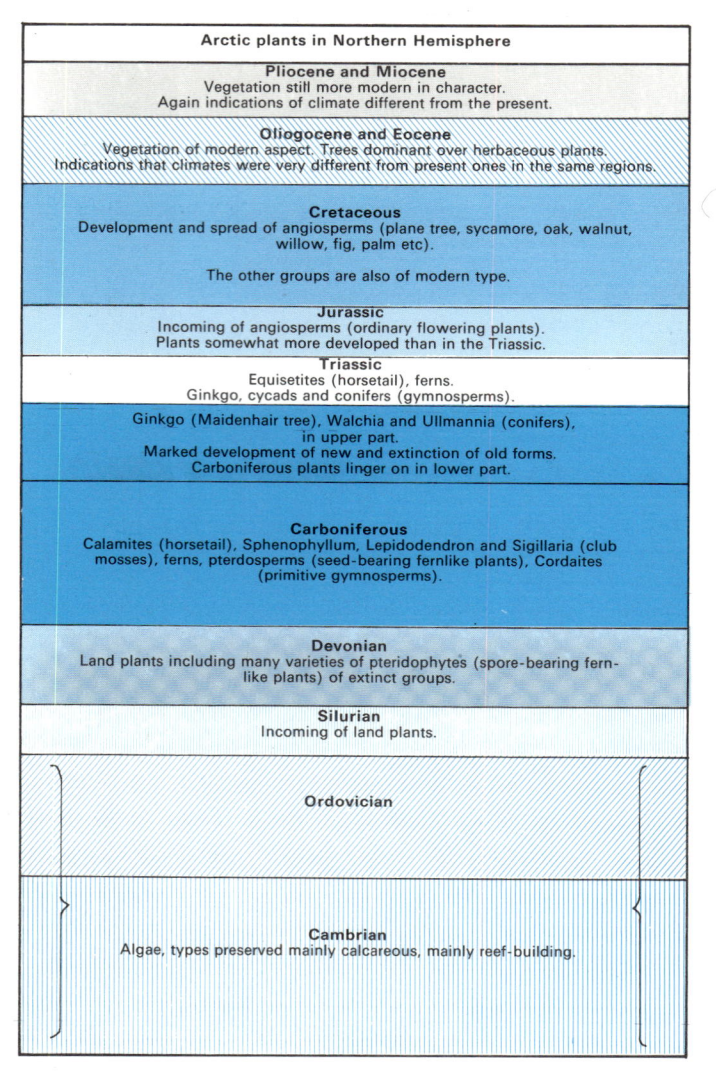

Arctic plants in Northern Hemisphere
Pliocene and Miocene Vegetation still more modern in character. Again indications of climate different from the present.
Oliogocene and Eocene Vegetation of modern aspect. Trees dominant over herbaceous plants. Indications that climates were very different from present ones in the same regions.
Cretaceous Development and spread of angiosperms (plane tree, sycamore, oak, walnut, willow, fig, palm etc). The other groups are also of modern type.
Jurassic Incoming of angiosperms (ordinary flowering plants). Plants somewhat more developed than in the Triassic.
Triassic Equisetites (horsetail), ferns. Ginkgo, cycads and conifers (gymnosperms).
Ginkgo (Maidenhair tree), Walchia and Ullmannia (conifers), in upper part. Marked development of new and extinction of old forms. Carboniferous plants linger on in lower part.
Carboniferous Calamites (horsetail), Sphenophyllum, Lepidodendron and Sigillaria (club mosses), ferns, pterdosperms (seed-bearing fernlike plants), Cordaites (primitive gymnosperms).
Devonian Land plants including many varieties of pteridophytes (spore-bearing fern-like plants) of extinct groups.
Silurian Incoming of land plants.
Ordovician
Cambrian Algae, types preserved mainly calcareous, mainly reef-building.

The chart '600 million years of Earth History' (produced by the Education Services of Esso Petroleum Company) is a useful aid for relating extinct and living creatures to this time scale. Children will find that man appears late in the earth's history. They could be encouraged to examine copies of the Lascaux cave paintings to find the type of animals early human beings hunted. The experience of trying to turn pieces of flint into spearheads by chipping will give some idea of the skill people of so long ago acquired in coming to terms with their prehistoric environment.

Following changes with the seasons

Older primary school children will already be aware of seasonal changes.

In the year before they transfer to middle or secondary school, they might use some of their time out of doors in collecting more precise information.

This could involve regular observation at intervals from September to July of the same 10-metre square. The same trees, garden flowers, weeds on the garden plot, birds and the games children play could also be studied in this way.

A group might study the same route in September, January, March and June successively, each time (as described in Volume 2 Part 1, pages 16–19) searching for the most common flowering and flowerless plants, birds sighted and heard, human activities and any other features of special interest. If records of their discoveries are displayed side by side, the seasonal changes will be as obvious as the changes corresponding to different types of soil mentioned on page 49.

What is the land made of?

Any of the following explorations and activities may increase children's interest in the actual materials of which the land is made. On many previous occasions rocks and pebbles will have been among the things children have sorted and tested, but it is now time for more searching comparisons emphasising the great variety of these things.

A good geological collection should be available in the school's resources centre for first-hand investigation whenever required. This can help to reduce the indiscriminate over-collecting of rocks.

Soil investigation
What is soil? Members of the class could carry out their investigations on different soils such as alluvium, loam, peat and sand.

Here are some possible lines of inquiry.

1. Magnify and look at broken rock fragments, pebbles, rotting material, very fine single particles or groups stuck together (crumb structure).

2. Feel whether the material is damp or dry, smooth or sharp; and whether it may stain fingers because of the chemicals it contains.

3. Dry out 100 g of soil until no further loss in mass occurs. Loss in mass represents the amount of water in the soil which was freely available to plants and animals.

4. Air is pushed out of spaces between soil crumbs or particles when water moves in.

Screw a straight-sided tin into the soil. Then dig it up and lower it into a tank; gently run water down the side of the tank until the tin is covered. What leaves the tin?

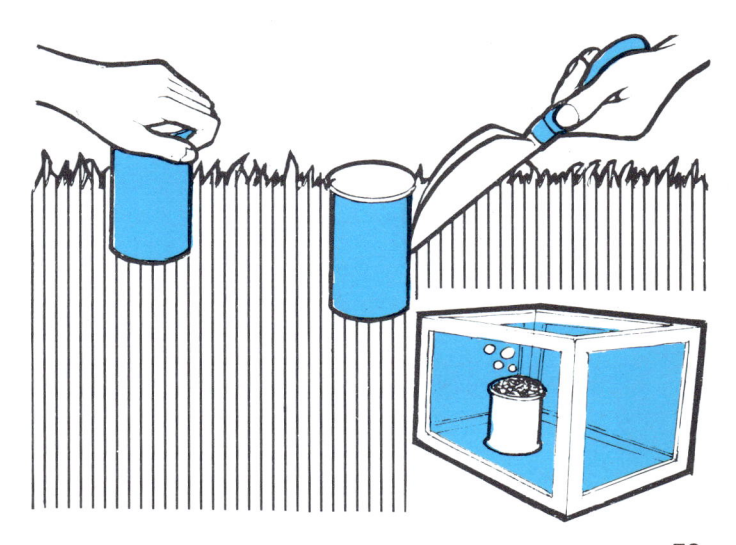

5. Burning will remove the organic parts of decaying plants and animals. Any minerals that were in their bodies will be left as ash with other minerals that were in the soil. For children of this age it is enough to say that the loss of mass is due to the loss of things that were once living, and that substances that were never alive are left.

Take 100 g of air-dried soil and heat it very strongly until red-hot. Continue heating until no further loss in mass occurs.

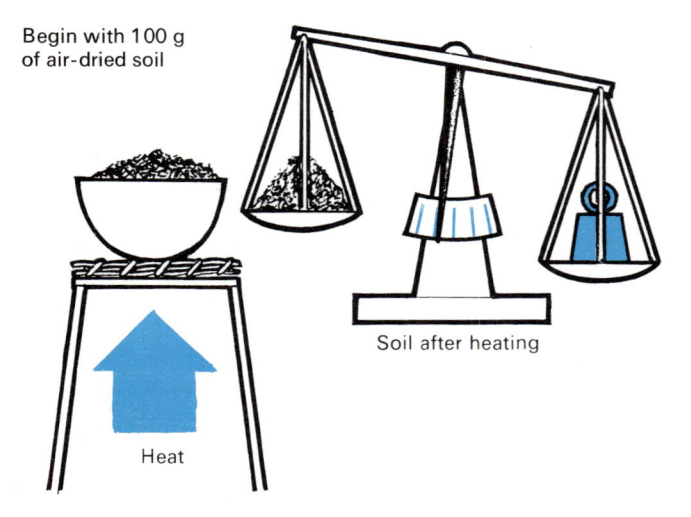

Begin with 100 g of air-dried soil

Soil after heating

Heat

These observations should help children to suggest that soil is not a single material, but something in which solid things such as particles of different rocks and rotting remains of many things once alive have become mixed with air and water.

An active search for some causes of change in rocks and dead material would be the best way of following up this idea.

Changes caused by mechanical action
Evidence from the beach
Collect a small bucket of shingle from the beach. Shake this through meshes of different sizes, such as a garden sieve, a colander, a mesh sieve, a tea strainer.

Glue the particles separated out in this way in order of size on to a board 6×45 cm in size.

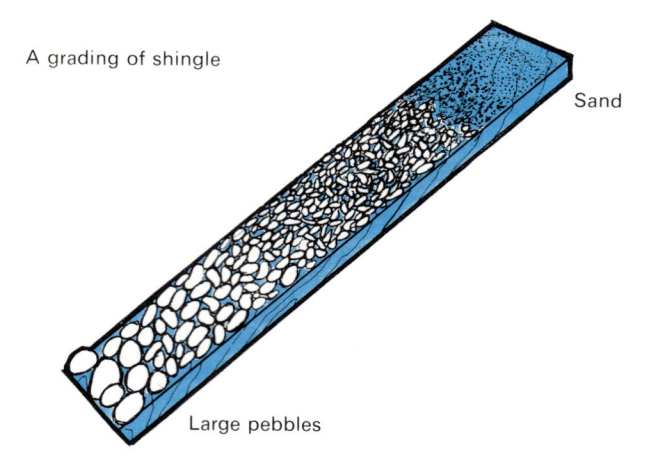

A grading of shingle

Sand

Large pebbles

Examine the pieces from all parts of the board with the aid of a stereomagnifier. Do the differently sized particles consist of similar materials?

If the only difference in these particles is one of size, it is reasonable to suggest that they all come from the same rocks that have been broken up by wave action.

Evidence of frost action
A very cold spell is a good time to find out more about the action of frost. Leave the arrangement of apparatus (seen in the illustration) out of doors throughout the night.

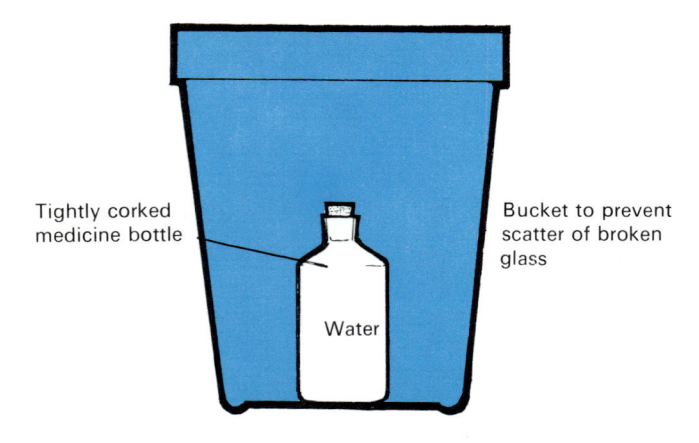

Tightly corked medicine bottle

Water

Bucket to prevent scatter of broken glass

If water in the cracks in rocks, bricks and roads freezes, it is likely that sufficient force is exerted to widen the cracks and so break up the mass.

Are rocks affected by plants?
Can you find any plants widening cracks in rocks or between bricks?

Scrape some lichen off a piece of rock. Is the surface beneath worn?

Is there any connection between the dates on the tombstones and the extent to which their stone is covered by lichen? Compare tombstones made of the same materials.

Changes caused by decay
Children can begin their investigations by trying to discover the conditions under which things that have been living decay most rapidly.

Suitable materials to use are pieces of apple, carrot, bread, lettuce and cabbage leaves, fallen leaves and milk.

Compare the effects of leaving similar masses of these things:

In dry states.
Moistened with tap water.
Moistened with rain water.
Immersed in rain water.
In containers with and without lids.
In cold and warm places.

What changes take place? When do they occur most rapidly?
Is there any evidence of anything causing any of the changes seen?

Occasionally a small dead animal such as a bird fallen from a nest or a mouse may be found.

One way of observing what happens to the animal is to bury it in damp garden soil in a wormery, allowing its body to remain visible through the glass. It can be left out of doors and examined at regular intervals.

Another method is to place the body in a jam jar covered with fine mesh wire netting to prevent interference from other animals such as cats, and leave it in a hole in the ground.

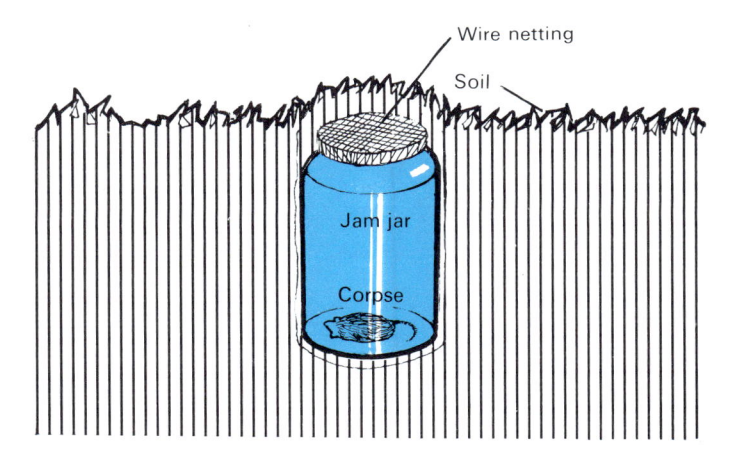

Does anything help the corpse to change?

Woodland litter consists of decaying material that has fallen from the trees. Collect samples of this material from the ground surface and from depths of 10 cm and 20 cm at the same spot. Make careful comparisons with the help of a stereomagnifier. Which sample consists of the smallest pieces?

It would be reasonable to expect the litter that had spent longest in the soil (ie that from the greatest depth) would be the most changed and probably therefore in smaller pieces. Much decay is due to the action of bacteria, but children would need to undertake some microbiological work to obtain more direct evidence that organisms other than the maggots and white worms they may have seen are continually at work changing material (see Nuffield *O-Level Biology, Students' Text no. 2*).

The following story gives some information about the rate at which dead material in the soil can be changed.

One autumn a few years ago a dead swan was discovered in the garden of a Wiltshire cottage. It probably died in flight and landed there by chance. The burial took place after the village policeman had been informed of its demise, which was necessary since swans are Crown property.

Someone thought that the bird's skeleton could serve as a useful teaching aid if it could be separated from the soft parts. Although this would be achieved by decay nobody had any idea of how long this would take, so the only way to find out was to fix a date for exhumation after what might be a reasonable period of time. The position of the grave was duly marked and a year later the digging and sifting of soil began. The guess proved successful and after about two hours' careful work most of the bones, even including the unexpectedly tiny axis and atlas vertebrae, had been collected. No sign of any flesh or feathers remained. The bleached and mounted bones were very interesting to many children.

Sorting the swan's bones

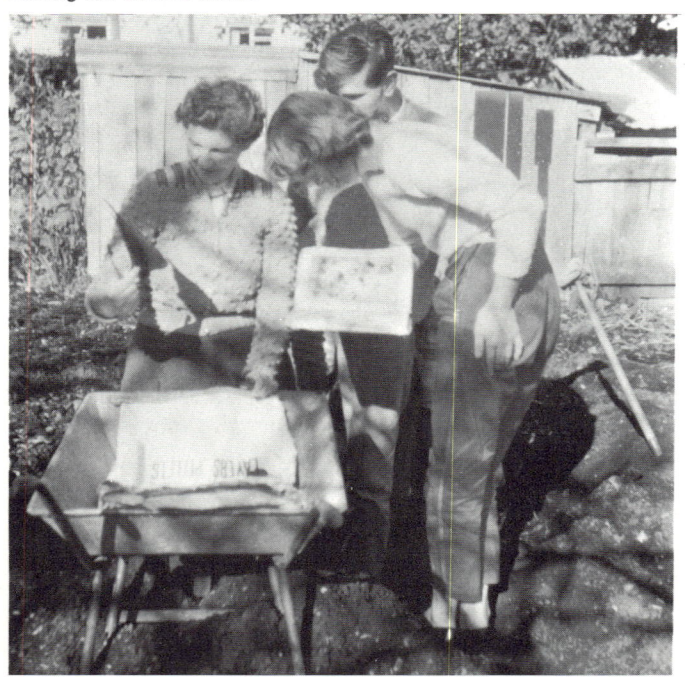

However, unsolved problems remain. Would a smaller animal become a skeleton more rapidly? Would the swan have decayed at the same rate at a different depth in the soil? Would the same type of things decay at different rates in different types of soil?

The action of earthworms in dragging plant material into the earth where the parts they do not eat can decay can also be investigated (see Nuffield *O-Level Biology, Students' Text no. 1*, pages 39–40 (Longman & Penguin, 1966).

Compost
Some children may like to find out more about the manufacture of compost from garden and kitchen waste. Some children may have noticed their fathers using a chemical substance called an activator for speeding up the process.

Make a mixture of refuse from chopped lettuce leaves, outer leaves of cabbage, potato peelings, grass cuttings, rotten apples and leaf litter.

Use two similar containers such as old aquaria or wide-necked sweet jars.

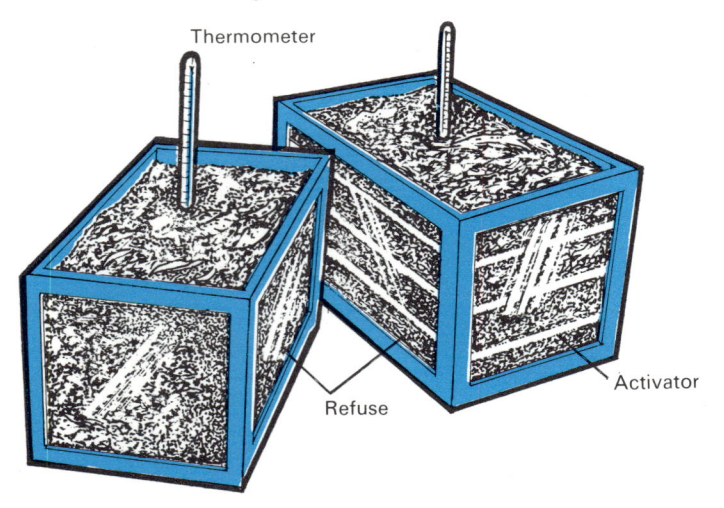

Fill one jar with refuse. In the other place layers of refuse 8–10 cm thick with some activating substance such as Garotta or sulphate of ammonia between each layer. If the refuse is very dry moisten it with a little water when placing it in the jars, but avoid soaking.

Place thermometers in similar positions in each jar.

Observe any visible decay through the sides of the jars.

Are there any smells? If so, how long did it take for these to become noticeable?

Keep comparative records of the temperatures in both jars from the time of setting up the investigation until decay is well advanced.

Decayed material in soil in known as *humus*. At this stage children could also be given these terms:

Organic, once part of living things.
Inorganic, substances that have never been living.

Organic and inorganic soils
Sand is a soil mainly consisting of inorganic particles and very little humus. Peat is mainly humus, and therefore organic, with very little broken rock.

The difference can be seen if the same amounts of sand and peat are shaken up with water and allowed to settle.

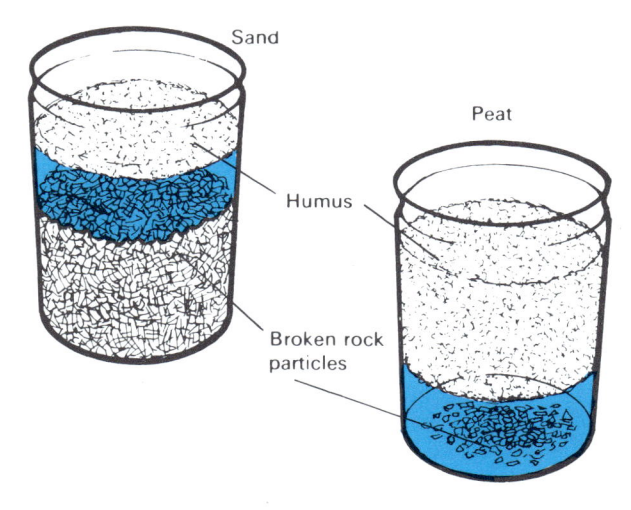

Another comparison of these two types of material is worth making.

Place 50 g of air-dried sand and air-dried peat in two tall funnels. Cover each with the same volume of water.

When this has drained through the materials, compare the quantities collected in the jars below.

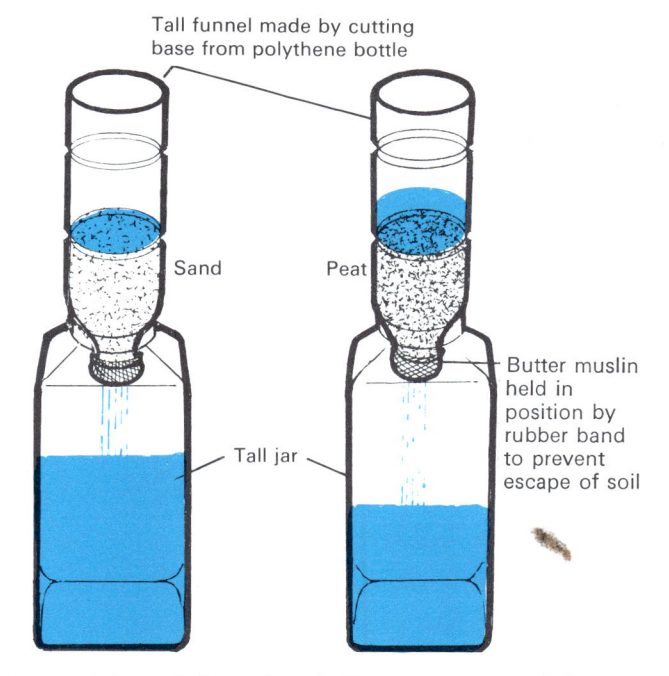

Now weigh each funnel and allow to stand and dry out. Which one does this most rapidly? That is, when can no further reduction in mass be detected? Which of these two soils might become waterlogged (with no spaces for air) in wet weather?

Which soil would contain plenty of air and no water during a dry spell?

Would a soil that is a mixture of rock particles and humus give the best conditions for growing plants?

Children can try to answer this question by growing the same numbers of the same plants in sand, peat and sand with peat.

What makes rocks and soils different?
As children examine and test the soils they find in different places, they should gradually become more aware of how much they vary, even though similar breaking-down processes have been involved in their formation.

The key to this puzzle lies in the fact that rocks, like soils, consist of different materials, brought together by changes involving movement and mixing in the course of many millions of years. After molten mixtures of minerals cooled to form the most ancient (igneous) rocks of the world such as granite and basalt, pieces were broken from them by weathering, then moved and mixed by forces exerted by various natural phenomena, and then deposited again as layers of sediment at the bottom of shallow seas. There they slowly became cemented together to form new (sedimentary) rock formations such as sandstones and shales. Hard skeletal parts of animals and different chemicals precipitated from water also settled to form other sedimentary rocks such as chalk and limestones. From time to time both the ancient and more recent rocks were changed again by conditions like great heat or pressure, and so became metamorphic (changed) rocks. Slate (from shale), marble (from limestone) and gneiss (from granite) are examples.

Soils are likely to bear close relationships to the rocks from which they have been formed. Therefore they will also be different from each other. The various quantities of humus, air and water that also become part of these soils simply increase the differences.

Children can only become aware of this and find it convincing if their experience in the countryside and in school enables them to collect evidence of these moving and mixing processes that are still changing rocks and soils in the way that has continued throughout geological time.

The action of other agencies upon the soil: moving and mixing

What does the wind do to the soil?
What stings the face on a dry windy day, especially on a sandy beach?

How has the cliff face become worn and uneven? Drive a post into the ground. Either attach a fly-paper to the upper part facing the prevailing wind, or coat this surface with Vaseline.
Does the material adhering to the sticky surface include any particles of soil?

These observations can provide evidence of the wind's power to move small particles. What about changes on a larger scale?

Try to collect some information about the amount of moving and mixing that can be achieved by the strong winds of tropical cyclones and hurricanes.

What is the Dust Bowl of America?

Wind eroded rocks

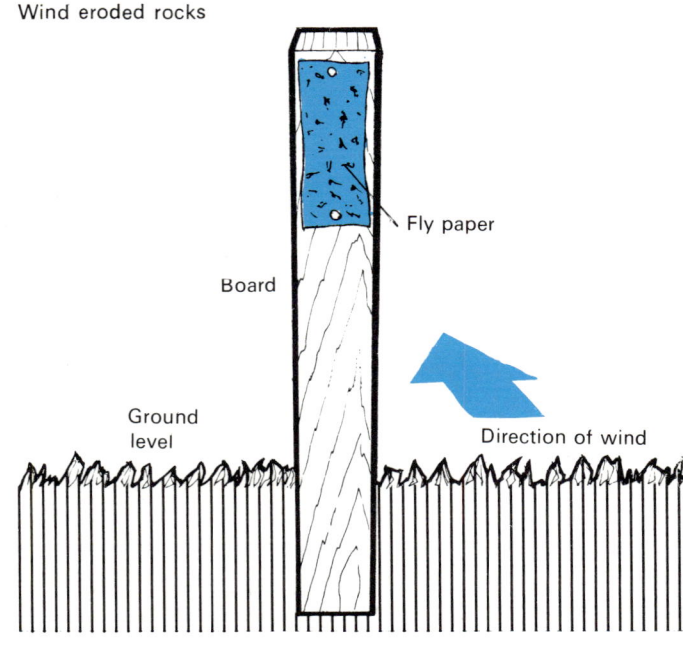

What does water do to the soil?
Moving
Filter some water from rivers and streams.
Look in gutters after heavy rain.
Examine places where puddles have dried up.
Follow a small twisting stream and draw a cross-section at each twist.

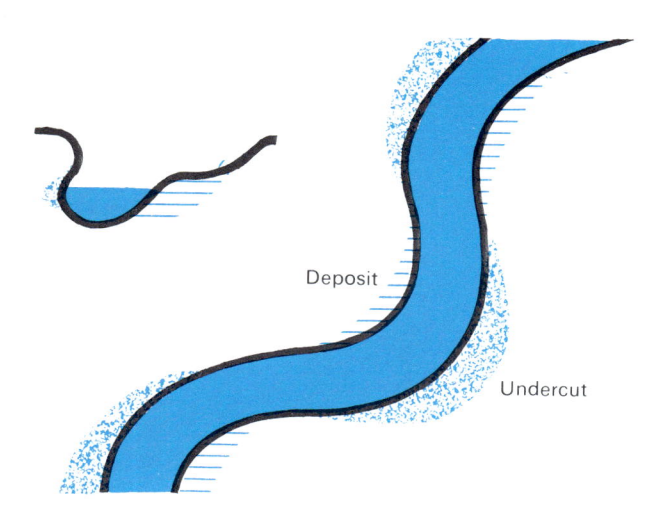

What is happening to the banks of the stream at these places?
What has water done over the years to the landscape and rocks in this photograph?

Children can easily collect evidence of water changing the position of soil. This is called erosion. Certain circumstances can increase or reduce this sort of movement.

Fill three boxes of the same size with the same type of soil and place buckets at one end of each.
Sow one with grass and tilt gently.
Tilt one gently. Tilt one steeply.
Pour the same quantity of water from the same height into each box.

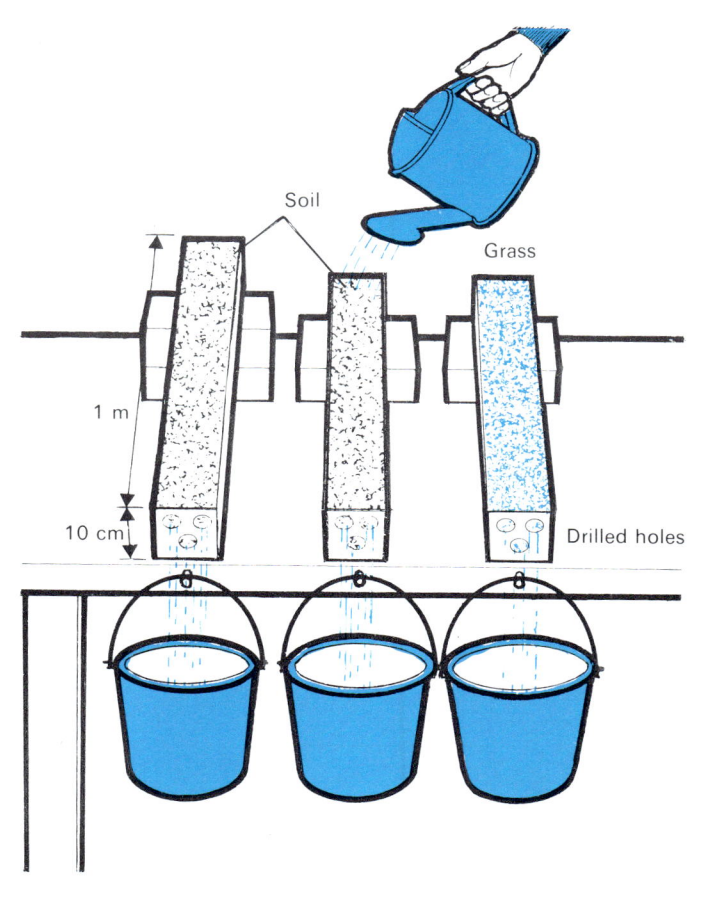

Compare the amounts of soil washed into the buckets.

This would be a good time to consider the direction of ploughing on hillsides; and to talk about the **Tennessee Valley Project**.

Depositing

When soil is shaken with water and then allowed to stand for some hours, particles settle in order of size.

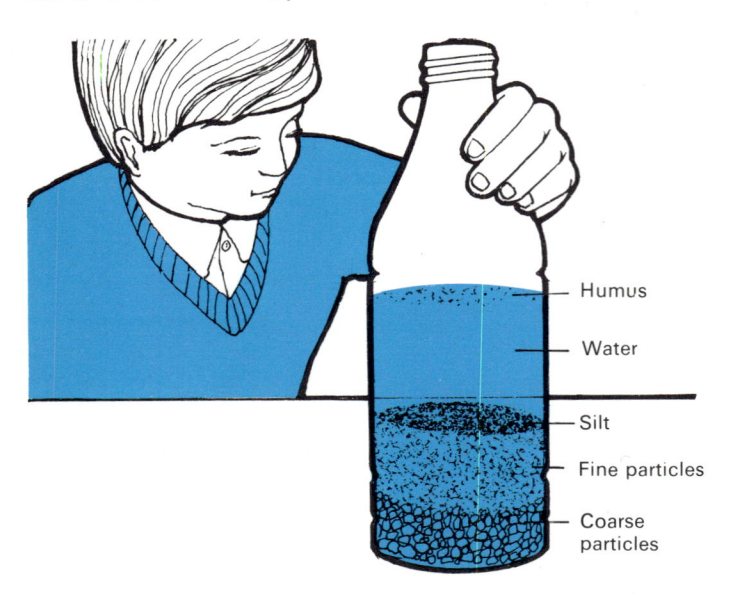

When children have discovered this, they can imagine how streams and rivers move particles of rocks and soils distances according to size.

Careful examination of rocks that have been formed by the cementing together of such particles will soon show this variation.

What has this to do with the formation of the great deltas of the world?

By how much is the shingle at Dungeness or Chesil Beach increasing each year?

What are moraines?

What do animals do to the soil?

Set up a wormery with layers of differently coloured moist soils. Place three or four earthworms on the surface. Examine the apparatus regularly during the following two or three weeks for signs of any alterations in the position of the soil. A thin layer of finely powdered white expanded polystyrene placed in the middle of the soil will serve as a good marker.

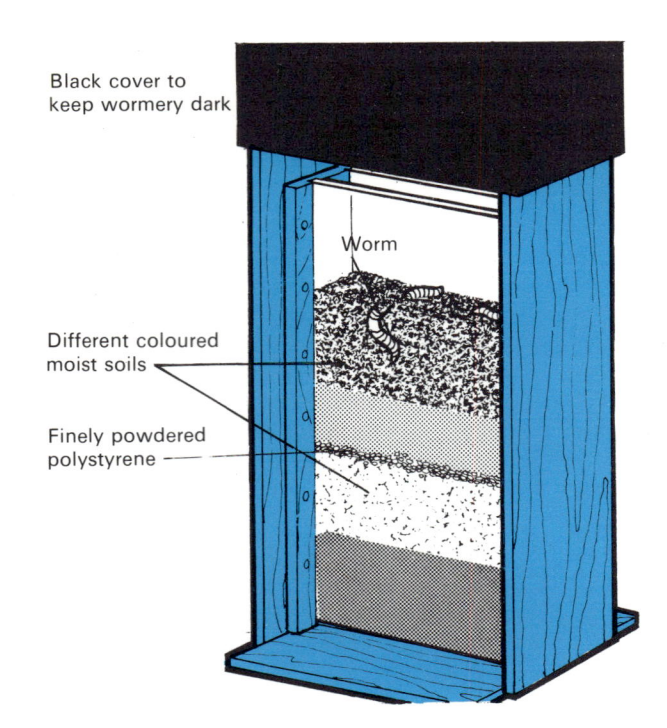

Specimens of a mole and its skeleton might be carefully examined perhaps during a museum visit, for the adaptations that enable it to be an efficient tunneller. (See Volume 3 Part 1, pages 62–63 for further details.)

See *School Projects in Natural History,* no. 1, pages 7 and 14, for further suggestions for fieldwork on the digging activities of moles. This booklet can be obtained from the Devon Trust for Nature Conservation, Slapton Ley Field Centre, Kingsbridge, Devonshire.

Information can also be collected about other animals that dig holes from gamekeepers, museums and reference books.

Men, machines and the soil

Man's earth-moving and mixing activities can provide children with many profitable lines of inquiry or a possible centre of interest.

Why does man dig holes?

The short answer is to get something out of the earth or to put something into it.

1. What materials does man take from the land?

Try to discover more about the mining of metallic minerals such as copper, iron ore and nickel.

How are non-metals such as salt, sulphur, graphite, quartz obtained? What are some of the uses of these materials?

On a map of the British Isles mark places where man obtains granite, limestone, ragstone, millstone grit, flint; clay, gault clay and chalk; sand and gravel. How are these materials used in the construction of buildings, bridges and roads?

What aids to communication come from removing soil and rocks? (Roads and tunnels.) What is the Mersey Mole? Do we need a Channel tunnel?

Peat, coal, oil and natural gas are known as sources of power. Can they all be obtained in the British Isles? Select one of these materials and try to describe in detail how man makes use of it.

Gems and clay are used to make beautiful objects. Can you collect some good examples?

Many things people used and wore long ago have been discovered underground. Can you name some famous archaeological discoveries of recent years and show how one of them has helped us to learn more about the past?

2. What does man put into the land?

What does he deposit and why?

When you visit a farm or walk through the park in spring, what do you see being put into the soil?

When you find a hole in the road, look down it. What has man put there? Why did he do this?

How do we get rid of rubbish and sewage? Try to find out more about this in your own district. How does man benefit?

What famous smugglers and pirates in literature have hidden valuable things in holes?

How does man change the soils he cultivates?
1. He adds air and improves drainage by digging and ploughing.

Begin with the same amounts of the same soil and the same quantities of water in two jam jars.

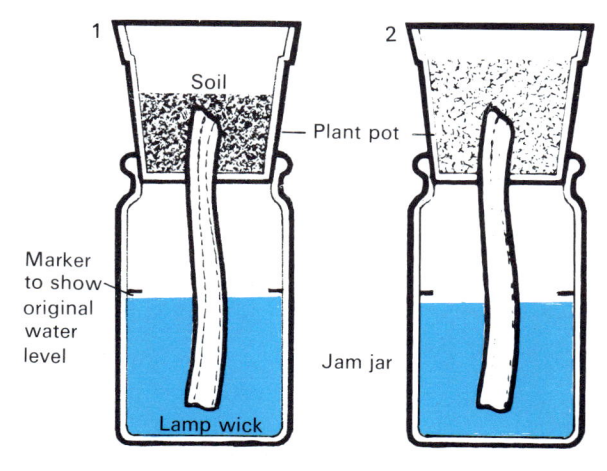

Dig the soil in pot no. 1 daily with a fork. Leave the soil in pot no. 2 untouched.

Why is water drawn up from jar no. 2 most rapidly?

(Air fills most of the spaces when the soil is dug regularly, so there is less room for water.)

Sow the same number of mustard seeds in two pots containing the same type of soil.

Plug the hole in pot no. 1 with a cork.

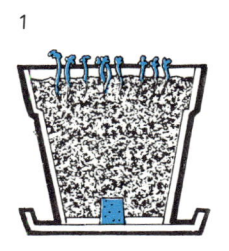

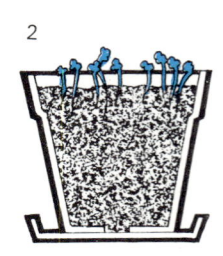

Water both pots well daily. After a fortnight uproot the plants, wash them and compare their heights, the sizes of their root systems and of their leaves.

Where was the greatest growth achieved, in waterlogged or well-drained soil?

2. He adds lime to lighten heavy clay soils.

Add a dessertspoonful of clay soil to two jars of water and shake.

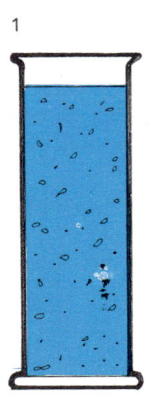

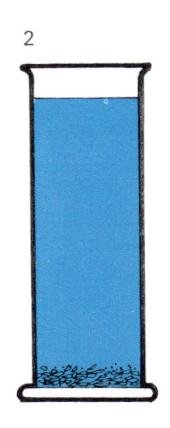

To jar no. 2 only, add $\frac{1}{4}$ teaspoonful of lime.

Allow each jar to stand for an hour.

Why does the water in jar no. 2 become much clearer?

(Lime causes the clay particles to come together in groups (flocculate) and thus become heavy and sink. Single particles of clay in jar no. 1 will still be in suspension.)

Flocculation creates more spaces for air between particles.

3. He increases the amount of humus by adding fertilisers.

Compare the growth of similar seeds in garden plots of the same size treated with horse dung, treated with a chemical fertiliser and untreated. The plots should not be adjacent as fertiliser may spread sideways.

Is it possible to add too much fertiliser to soil?

Food for thought
When we consider the rate at which man now carries out all these activities and make comparisons with what he could achieve a hundred, or two thousand, years ago it is clear that his power to change his surroundings by moving and mixing the earth's materials is growing as rapidly as his power to invent bigger and better machines to carry out the work.

Should this growth continue indefinitely?

Does this moving and mixing of materials always bring about improvements?

Does it affect wild creatures?

How long will the stocks of materials in the earth last? How rapidly are the numbers of people in the world requiring food increasing?

These are some of the questions conservationists are asking today. It is not too early for children of about eleven to be put in the way of experience that, in due course, may encourage them to think seriously about these questions too.

4 The children's playground as a centre of interest

'In one area of South London a huge extent of Thames marshland was until recently an ideal "lung" for children from the neighbouring suburbs. Here it was possible to light fires, dam streams, catch tadpoles and sticklebacks and take part in all kinds of adventurous play. Some of this area has already been drained, and is occupied by twelve thousand inhabitants. Work has started on dwellings to accommodate sixty thousand more, equivalent to a town the size of Guildford being erected on the edge of our largest city. Not only has this area been lost to the nearby children, but thousands more are coming to live on the site without natural play space of their own. The construction of municipal recreation grounds with swings, climbing frames and sand pits goes some way towards meeting the needs of the youngest children, but the play that can be observed there is different from the jungle play that was so common on the marshes. The reality of the adventure is missing and the chance to pick wild flowers gone. What can you say to a little girl who comes to school with a bunch of daffodils picked in a nearby Council wood and says innocently, "Some of 'em have still got their bottoms on"?' *

It requires little imagination to think of many more problems created by the spread of densely populated urban areas. Obviously we need more residential field centres if we are to compensate many children for lack of accessible countryside and help them to discover that observation of living things in their natural habitats can be much more interesting than picking and collecting flowers and creatures for no particular purpose.

Something can be done through links between schools. One good scheme was begun by the headmistress of a very small rural school in beautiful surroundings who invited a class from a neighbouring town to join her children for a day's work. The country children took their visitors to one of their favourite outdoor places and worked with them while the two teachers helped them all to think about what they saw and found. Equipment and reference books belonging to the host school were shared and arrangements made for the explorers to overflow from the small school building into the village hall for immediate follow-up work.

News of this expedition and the head teacher's willingness to help soon spread, and now ten urban schools are associated with this enterprising village group and plans are in hand for increasing the supply of equipment required for these efforts.

Advantages have not been limited to one direction. The village children have exchanged ideas with many more people than their rather isolated community can provide, and their awareness and understanding of their own surroundings have increased as they have tried to find the right words for comments to their visitors; and they now know where they will be welcome when they are ready to find out more about urban conditions.

Even when generous residential provision and good contacts between schools exist, urban children's opportunities for exploring open countryside can only be intermittent. This does not matter, for field studies can be done anywhere. We would wish urban children to have many experiences that help them to develop concern for their own surroundings and to know that any place contains something worth investigating whether it be a village pond, a hole in the road, or the great bridge taking the motorway across the river.

---

*Razzell, A. G., Juniors: a Postscript to Plowden (Penguin, 1968).

What starting points for inquiry can the urban children find in the swings and climbing frames on the municipal recreation ground that happens to be near their school? This tubular steel equipment firmly embedded in tarmac will not change with the seasons, it contains no undergrowth concealing small creatures, yet it is equipment that children use readily in giving themselves many different experiences. The situations they create in this way are worth thinking about and exploiting.

The equipment in the playground in the park has to stand up to much wear and tear, so it has to be strong. Much of it is made of tubular steel. Are tubes any stronger or weaker than solid rods of the same material and the same size? How could this be tested? (See Volume 2 Part 1, page 69.)

In how many ways can strips of Meccano be joined together to make strong, rigid shapes? How many rigid shapes can you discover in the playground in the park? (See the Unit *Structures and forces Stages 1 & 2*)

Beginning with a slide

Children in the playground can think of many questions that might be answered by having some slides.

Did you have to push off to start yourself sliding?
How long does one 'go' take?
Does an average of three 'goes' give a better time? Time the same child.
How long is the slide? Only measure the sloping part.
Does everybody take the same amount of time to travel this distance?

Does a girl travel quicker than a boy?

Can you work out your own speed in metres per second now that you know the length of the slope and the number of seconds you take coming down it?

Is there any speeding up or slowing down during the journey?
How could a faster slide be made?
Do the ways in which you sit or lie while sliding make any difference to the speed?
What happens when you try to slide sitting on mats of different materials? Try fibre PE mats, rubber and foam plastic bath mats, and both sides of a piece of carpet.
Which travels down the slide faster, a child or a ball such as a large rubber PE ball?
Watch the ball carefully as it travels. What happens to it that does not happen to you?

These experiences can give children plenty to think about and back in school investigations could continue with the help of models. A slide is after all only a slope with a smooth surface.

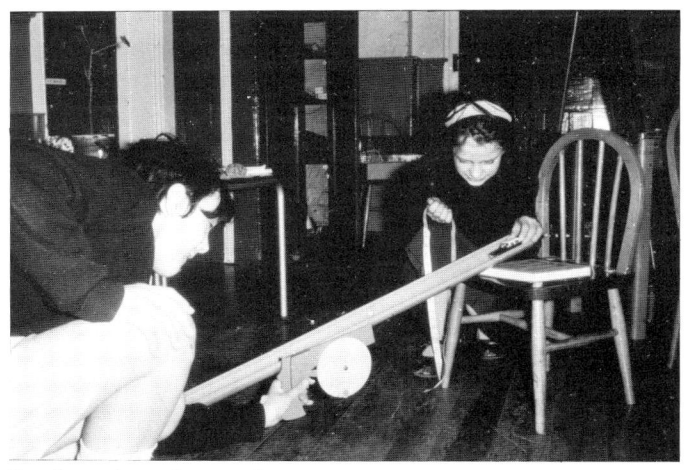

Sending a boat down a slope

Slopes
It could be interesting to find out what happens when slopes are altered and different things allowed to go down them.

Many things can be used for the next investigations. Children should not be hurried, they should be encouraged to use as many ideas as possible.

On the next page are some of the things they might think of using to make slopes:

Lengths of curtain track along which things can slide.

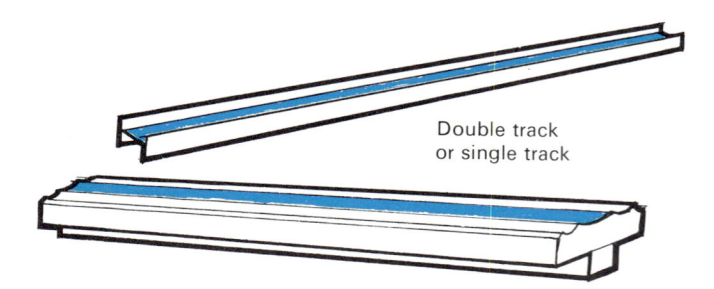

Double track or single track

Lengths of Marley guttering.

The slide in the outdoor play equipment of the infant department.

PE forms.

Strips of hardboard.

Lengths of nylon fishing line (monofilament).

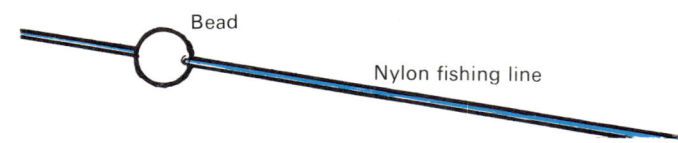

Bead
Nylon fishing line

Lengths of timber with one surface planed smooth or with a groove gouged out along its length.

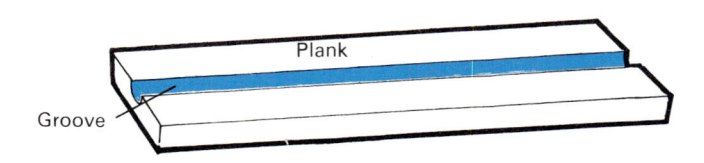

Plank
Groove

Moving things will tend to fall over the sides of forms or planks, so some restraining arrangement will be needed.

Stage blocks, boxes or clamps fixed to retort stands could be used for supporting these things in sloping positions.

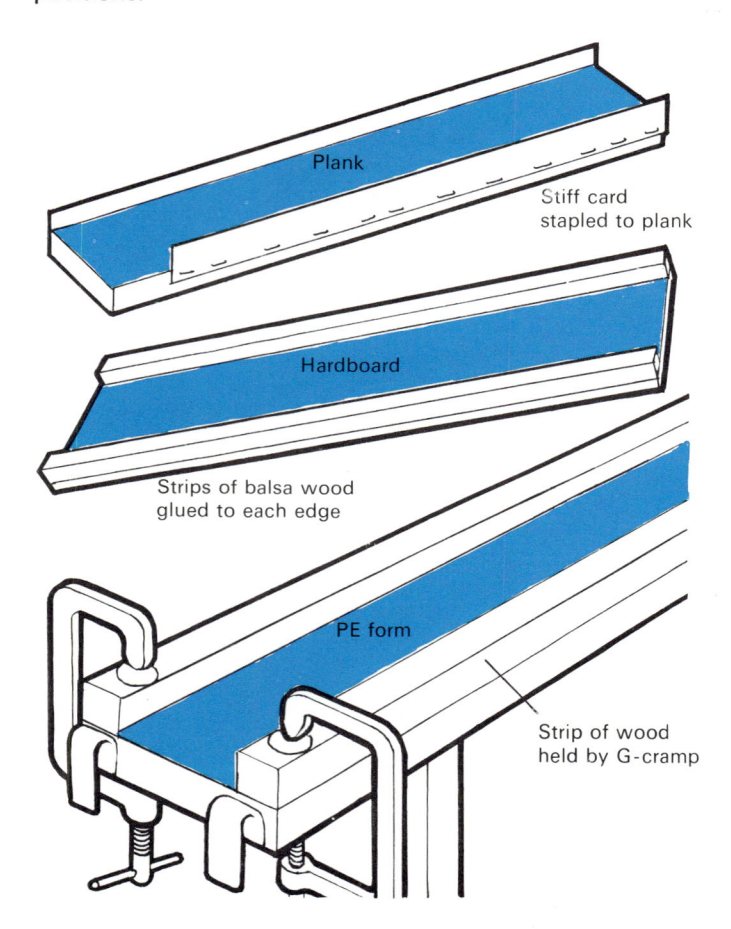

Plank
Stiff card stapled to plank

Hardboard
Strips of balsa wood glued to each edge

PE form
Strip of wood held by G-cramp

Some of these materials may prove to be springy as objects travel along them. This can give children opportunities to make additional interesting observations.

If this springy movement of a slope is not required it will need additional support underneath in order to make it rigid; or else a line will have to be pulled more tightly.

Planks of wood may warp, so lengths of chipboard (Weyroc) or thick plywood (2·5 cm) may prove more satisfactory.

Things to send down the slopes

Nylon glider with hook removed
Curtain track
Nylon fishing line (monofilament)
Small bulldog clip
Small runner made from inverted curtain glider
Beads of different sizes, shapes and materials

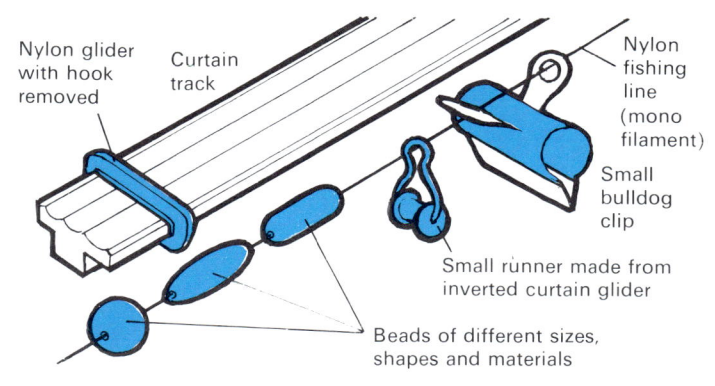

Small tins and boxes of different materials, some made heavier than others by filling with sand.
Balls; rubber, ping pong; glass marbles, ball bearings, etc.
Small toys with and without wheels.
Objects with both flat and curved surfaces such as cylindrical tins, corks, pencils, etc.
Pebbles (round, flat, oval).
Irregularly shaped things such as pieces of rock.

Children will need plenty of time to observe what happens and they should be encouraged to repeat their observations to check whether particular movements happen every time.

Slopes and objects can be changed around.

They should find it possible to sort objects according to their behaviour on the slopes.

Comparing sliding and rolling things
Some children may now like to undertake these investigations.

Which things go down the slope most rapidly? Take an average of three goes for each object.

Does the object's mass make any difference to its speed when it is a slider? When it is a roller?

Does the object's shape make any difference to its speed when it is a slider? When it is a roller?

What happens to sliders and rollers at the end of the slope?

What can you discover about the distances some things roll when they come off the slope? A long corridor with a smooth floor is a good place for trying this.
Does the steepness of slope make any difference to the distance of rolling?
Does the type of floor a thing rolls over make any difference to the distance it rolls? Place different surfaces at the foot of the slope and test with the same rolling object.

You will notice that rollers begin to move as soon as they are put on most slopes. Can you find any slope that does not set a roller moving?
What sort of slopes do sliders need before beginning to move?
Does the mass of the slider make any difference to the type of slope it needs for its movement to begin?

Things we put on the slope			
Rolling things	Sliding things	Things which could slide and roll	Things with mixed-up movements
Glass marble Rubber ball Wheels of car Round pebble	Flat pebble Matchbox Brick Unifix cube Bead Bulldog clip Nylon runner	Toilet roll Pencil Oval pebble	Bottle stoppers

Increasing the steepness of slopes

Consideration of this topic gives teachers and children plenty of scope for discussing some very useful scientific and mathematical ideas if the concepts involved can be illustrated in concrete ways.

It is appropriate to do this when children have had some previous experience of things of different sizes being proportional to each other and have met the idea of ratio.

The following equipment is required:

Four wooden laths or curtain track each 12 dm in length.

Ten 1-dm cubes (boxes 1 dm in height can be used). Some coloured tape.

Ask the children to set up a series of slopes with the 12-dm strips using an appropriate number of cubes or boxes to increase their rise by 1 dm each time.

With the help of Sellotape, fix coloured tape to these models in a way that draws attention to the fact that each time, as the rise between the lower and upper levels of these slopes increases, the distance over which one unit of that rise takes place decreases. See the table below.

Models of slopes becoming steeper	$\dfrac{\text{Length of whole slope}}{\text{Rise of whole slope}}$	Gradient	$\dfrac{L_1}{R_1} = \dfrac{L_2}{R_2}$
Gradient: rise of 1 dm in 12 dm	$12:1 = \dfrac{12}{1} = \dfrac{12}{1}$	1 in 12	
Gradient: rise of 1 dm in 6 dm	$12:2 = \dfrac{12}{2} = \dfrac{6}{1}$	1 in 6	
Gradient: rise of 1 dm in 4 dm	$12:3 = \dfrac{12}{3} = \dfrac{4}{1}$	1 in 4	
Gradient: rise of 1 dm in 3 dm	$12:4 = \dfrac{12}{4} = \dfrac{3}{1}$	1 in 3	

What is a gradient?

By skilful questioning and the help of the models teachers can try to help children to understand and talk about some of the following ideas.

The gradient of a slope is the distance (L_2), in whatever units we are measuring, that we must travel along the slope, in order to rise (or fall) a distance (R_2) equal to one of these same units.
The shorter the distance we have to travel in order to rise one unit, the steeper the slope.
The gradient of a slope can be found by dividing the length of the whole slope (L_1) by its total rise (R_1) because $\frac{L_1}{R_1}$ is proportional to $\frac{L_2}{R_2}$ (the gradient).
In other words L_1 is in the same ratio to R_1 as L_2 is to R_2.

A gradient is a ratio.

When we compare the gradients of different slopes we are comparing the same ratios for each one of them.

When a number of these ratios (gradients) are unlike, the steepness of the slopes they describe is also different.

As children become familiar with these ideas they could consolidate their understanding by trying to calculate gradients of other slides they know or could set up, eg:

The slide in the park.
Slides belonging to the outdoor play equipment.

Slopes with similar gradients

Slopes of different sizes with similar gradients

Children may find great difficulty in understanding how large and small slides and hills can have the same gradients. Again the way to understanding is through concrete experience. A working group will probably find that the school hall or playground will be the best place for this investigation.

Attach a cup hook to one end of pieces of string or tape 60, 48, 36, 24, 12 and 3 dm in length.

Screw these cup hooks into a post the following distances above the ground with the longest tape highest and the other pieces in decreasing order of length: 20, 16, 12, 8, 4, 1 dm.

Place the free ends of these tapes to touch the ground when pulled taut. Secure them in that position by attaching them to the tops of metal meat skewers driven into the ground. The children will find they have made another series of slopes.

If children are encouraged to make some comparisons they can discover that all the slopes in this series form, with the ground, triangles similar in shape and proportional to each other in size. The ratio of the length of slope to its rise is the same for each slope. Therefore their gradients are also similar.

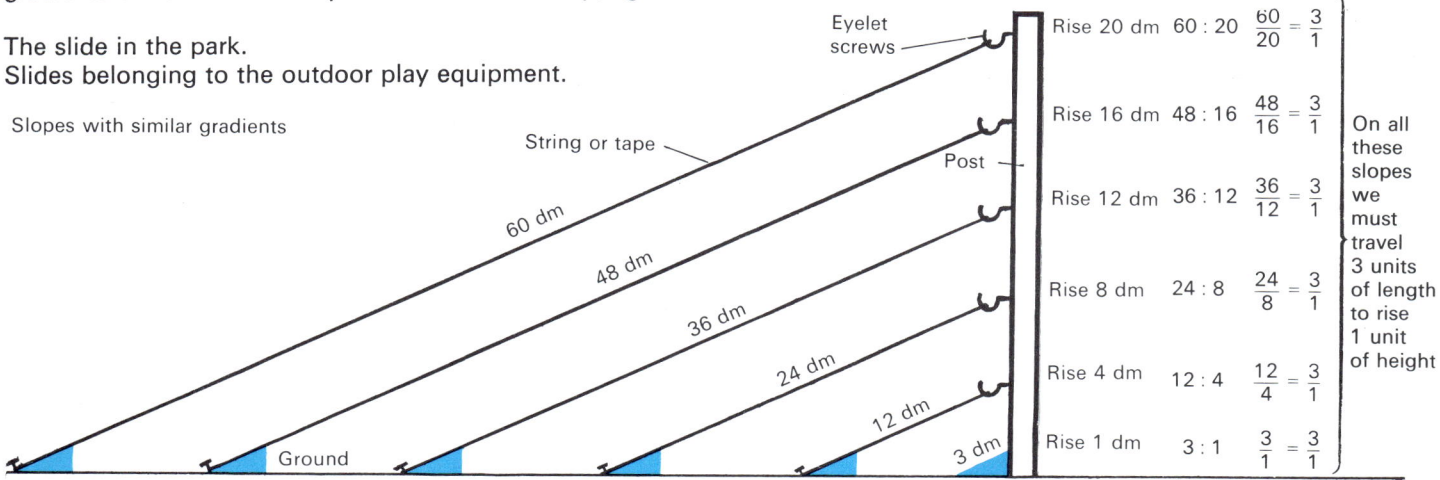

Rise 20 dm	60 : 20	$\frac{60}{20} = \frac{3}{1}$
Rise 16 dm	48 : 16	$\frac{48}{16} = \frac{3}{1}$
Rise 12 dm	36 : 12	$\frac{36}{12} = \frac{3}{1}$
Rise 8 dm	24 : 8	$\frac{24}{8} = \frac{3}{1}$
Rise 4 dm	12 : 4	$\frac{12}{4} = \frac{3}{1}$
Rise 1 dm	3 : 1	$\frac{3}{1} = \frac{3}{1}$

On all these slopes we must travel 3 units of length to rise 1 unit of height

All these slopes have a gradient 1 in 3

If the children compare this series of slopes with the previous series of models constructed with laths and blocks they should be helped to appreciate the difference between a set of slopes with the same gradients and another set with different gradients.

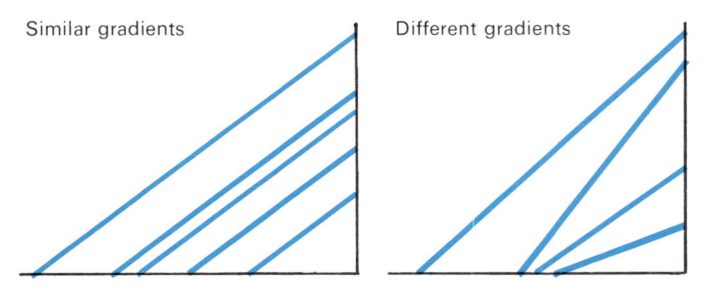

Similar gradients   Different gradients

They could also draw diagrams of slopes with similar and different gradients on squared paper. Measurements can be made in any units for calculation of a gradient, as long as the length of the slope and its rise are in the same units.

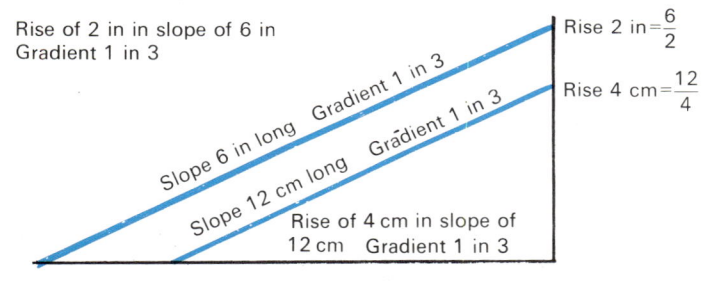

Rise of 2 in in slope of 6 in
Gradient 1 in 3

Rise 2 in $= \frac{6}{2}$

Slope 6 in long   Gradient 1 in 3

Rise 4 cm $= \frac{12}{4}$

Slope 12 cm long   Gradient 1 in 3

Rise of 4 cm in slope of 12 cm   Gradient 1 in 3

Changing slopes
The slope of a slide is regular but the slopes of hills and mountains are often steep in some places and gentle in others.

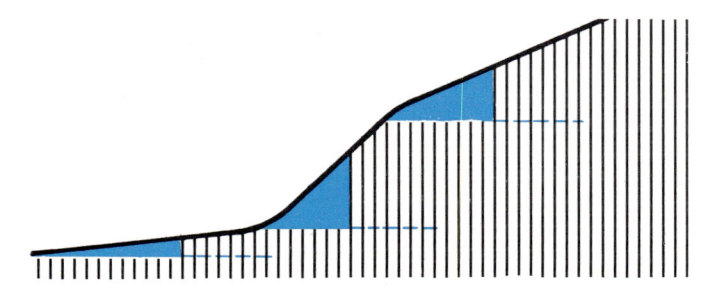

How could we find out more about these slopes?

Friction
As they investigate slides and slopes children will often find something that seems to be interfering with their own movement or the motion of some objects. Here are some examples.

Sitting on mats of certain materials makes travelling down the slide in the park difficult.
If a small box is placed at the top of a slope, made only just steep enough to set it sliding, it moves along slowly, at times almost stops, then continues on its way again. When a ball is allowed to roll off a slope and on to flat surfaces covered by different materials it is brought to a stop much sooner on some surfaces than on others.
What about watching a school caretaker at work?
Does he have a struggle pushing heavy things around?
Does he find ways of making the work easier?
How would mother get on with the housework if there were no castors on some of the furniture?

When observation and direct experience has convinced children that there is force opposing motion—*the force exerted by friction*—it is time to find out more about it. Then they may like to use a piece of equipment like this.

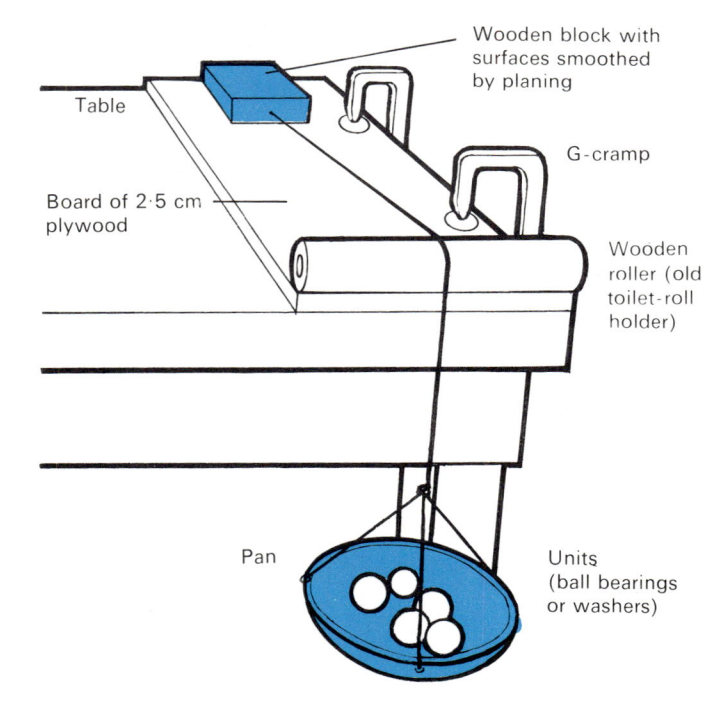

Wooden block with surfaces smoothed by planing

Table

G-cramp

Board of 2·5 cm plywood

Wooden roller (old toilet-roll holder)

Pan

Units (ball bearings or washers)

70

The more friction there is between the block of wood and the board, the greater will be the pull required to keep the block moving along the board.
The force of gravity exerts a pull on the pan and its contents and this, in turn, pulls on the string attached to the wooden block. Therefore the number of units in the pan sufficient to keep the block moving along steadily, can serve as an arbitrary measure of the frictional force opposing its motion.

Children can alter conditions affecting the block and the board and then test to find out whether they have increased or reduced friction. (Please note that no mention has been made of the effect of *inertia*. At this stage it may confuse the children while they are trying to develop ideas about friction.)

What increases or reduces friction?
How many units are required to keep the block moving during the following tests?

1. With one surface of the block in contact with the board, tow the block on its broad side and on its narrow side.

2. Tow the block along loaded with different masses: 100, 200, 300 grammes, etc.

3. Collect a wide range of materials to tack on to the under surface of the block and the surface of the board, eg: various fabrics, metal foil, polythene, rubber, carpet, sandpaper (different grades), blotting paper, smooth card.

Try towing the block with similar and with different materials in contact.

4. Some materials, like polythene, will stick together when in contact. Spread a liquid such as oil, liquid detergent or water, over the surface of the board. Then tow the block along. Which of these liquids is the best lubricant?

Some powders, such as French chalk, could also be rubbed on the board. The same test can then be carried out.

Lubricants get between the spaces on rough surfaces and prevent interlocking.

Struggling to move a stage block

Making it easier with rollers

5. Set some rollers made out of dowel rod beneath the block. How does their rolling reduce friction?

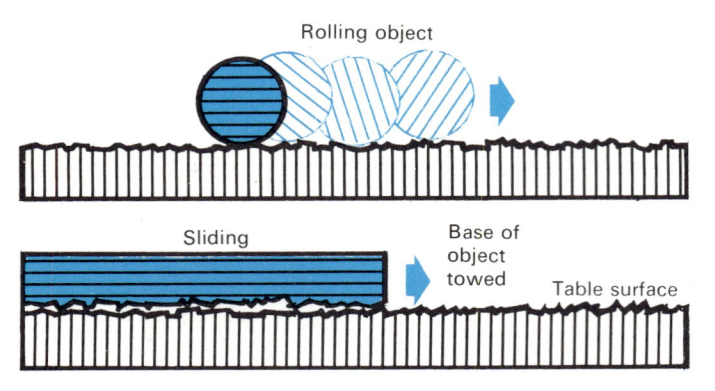

Rolling object

Sliding — *Base of object towed* — *Table surface*

The roller moves by turning over and over on the rough surface. When the block alone is towed over the table surface, the projections on both surfaces interlock and cause friction. Even when the surfaces in contact appear smooth, there are projections on them that can interlock.

What is the disadvantage of using rollers beneath a cart?

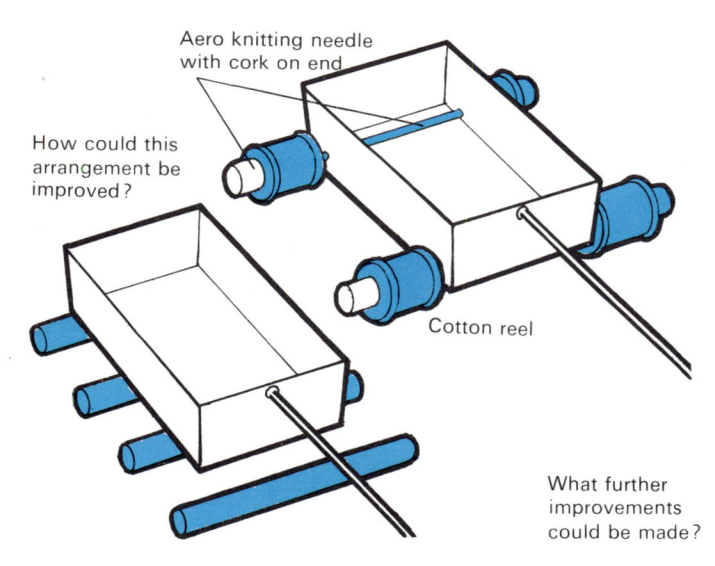

Aero knitting needle with cork on end

How could this arrangement be improved?

Cotton reel

What further improvements could be made?

When children have had enough experience with balls, rollers and lubricants to know that many things move more easily when friction has been reduced, it is quite possible that somebody may ask what would happen if we could get rid of friction altogether.

This idea could be investigated by making model hovercrafts. Some suggestions about doing that can be found in *Holes, gaps and cavities Stages 1 & 2*, Science 5/13, page 17 (Macdonald Educational, 1973), and in *Make and Find Out*, Book 4 (Macmillan, 1970).

What happens when these models are set in motion by a push across a smoothly polished horizontal surface?

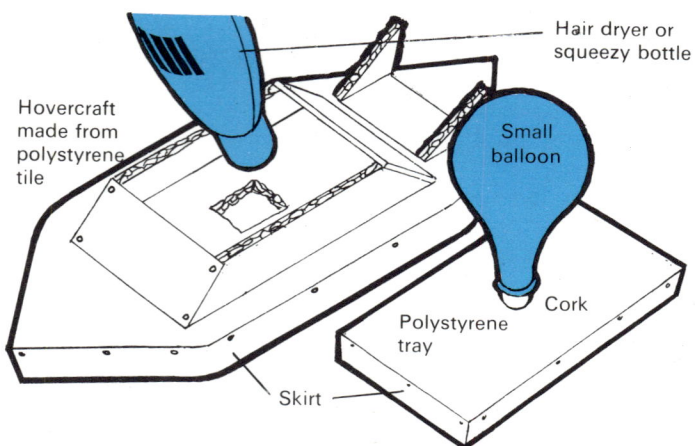

Hair dryer or squeezy bottle

Hovercraft made from polystyrene tile

Small balloon

Cork

Polystyrene tray

Skirt

Some children could also try to find out how far balls will continue their travels across a smooth polished floor after running down a slope inclined at an angle of not less than 30°.

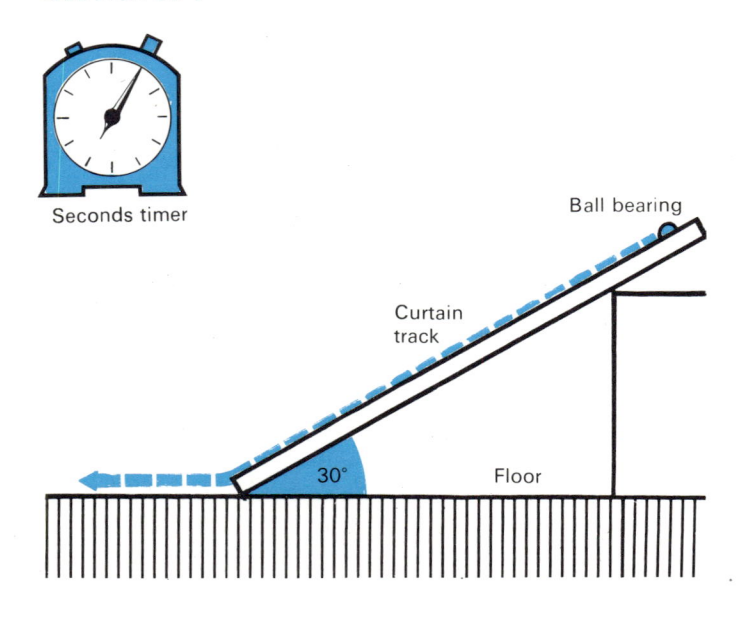

Seconds timer

Ball bearing

Curtain track

30°

Floor

72

It is unlikely that children can go much further with work along these lines until a later stage, but teachers need to know why this initial experience of friction is so important.

For more than two thousand years man mistakenly believed that things needed pushing or pulling, the application of force, to keep them moving. It is easy now to understand how this error arose. Some things when set in motion are very quickly brought to a standstill by the opposing force of friction, and so need pushing again.

The scientist Galileo Galilei (1564–1642) studied the movement of balls after they came to the end of their journeys down slopes. His results helped to pave the way for Sir Isaac Newton's (1642–1727) work on motion. This established the possibility that once things have been set in motion force is not required to keep them going.

The effect of applying pushes or pulls is to *change* the motion of the moving thing, either by slowing it down, speeding it up or by making it change its direction. It is necessary to be aware of this in order to understand modern dynamics. Therefore some early experience of situations involving and lacking friction will set children on the right track towards later progress.

Can friction be useful?

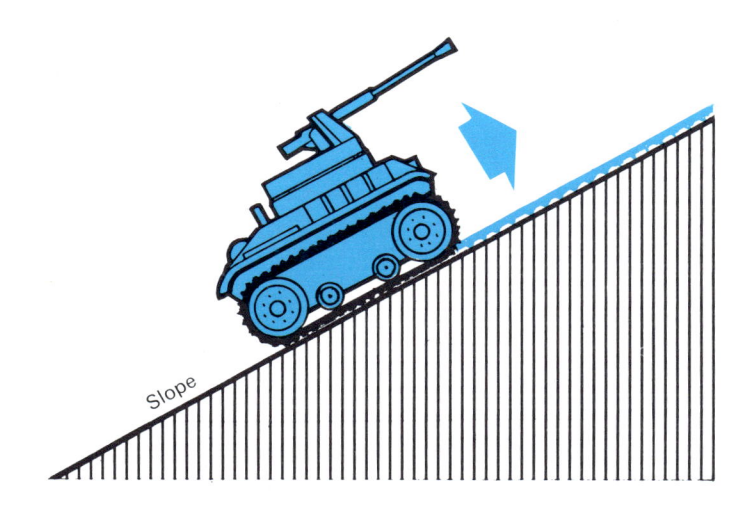

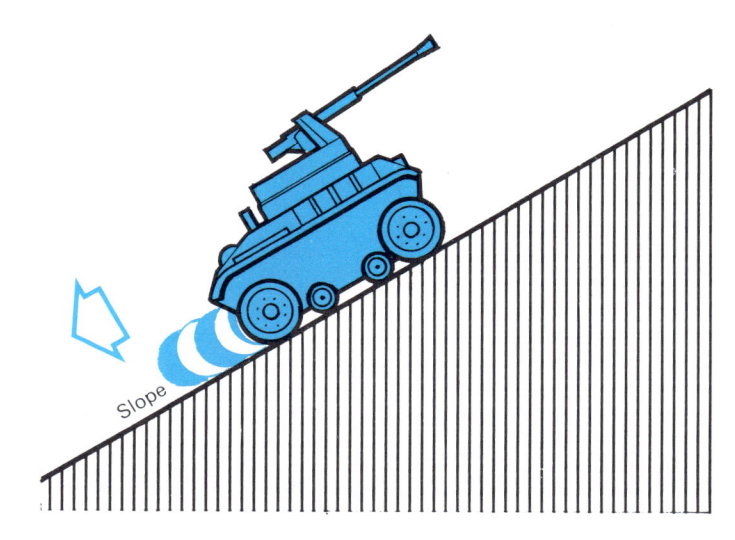

What happens when clockwork tanks climb a slope with and without their caterpillar tracks?

How do brakes slow up bicycles and cars?

Why do we grit icy roads?

Increasing speed

Some children after sliding in the park may like to try to find out whether things really do travel faster and faster as they go down a slope.

This is not easy to test owing to the difficulty of timing things that travel quickly over short distances. However, quite long slopes (6–8 metres) can be made with the aid of nylon fishing line (monofilament). If a small Bulldog clip is threaded on to this it will slide along with practically no interference from friction when the angle of the slope is not less than 25°.

A good deal of space is required for this work, so the best places for doing it are school halls and corridors. It can also be done out of doors on calm days. At other times wind resistance can slow down the speed of the sliding object.

Two possible ways of finding out whether there are any increases in the slider's speed can be discussed with the children. They can check their results by trying both ways.

The first method involves finding the time taken by the slider to make journeys of 2, 4 and 6 metres down the slope (an average of three goes each time). By subtraction it is then possible to find out whether the time taken to cover the 3rd and 4th metres and then the 5th and 6th metres decreases, as it should if the slider's speed increases.

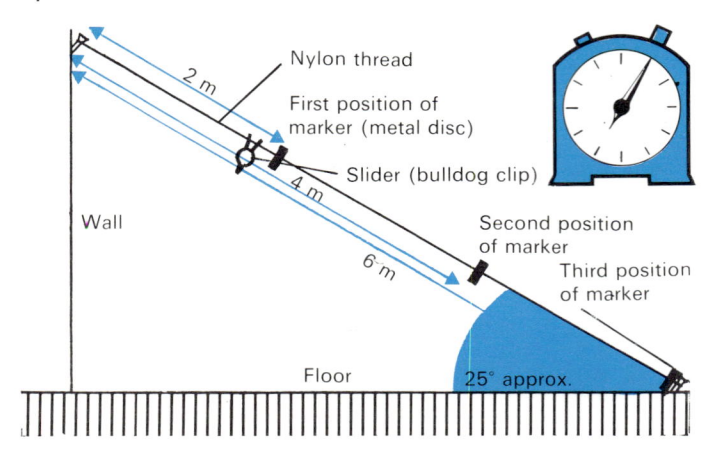

The slider's movements are easier to time if it can hit a marker so that a sound can be heard at the end of each run. A good way of arranging this is by attaching a small metal disc from a Meccano set to the required positions on the slope with Sellotape.

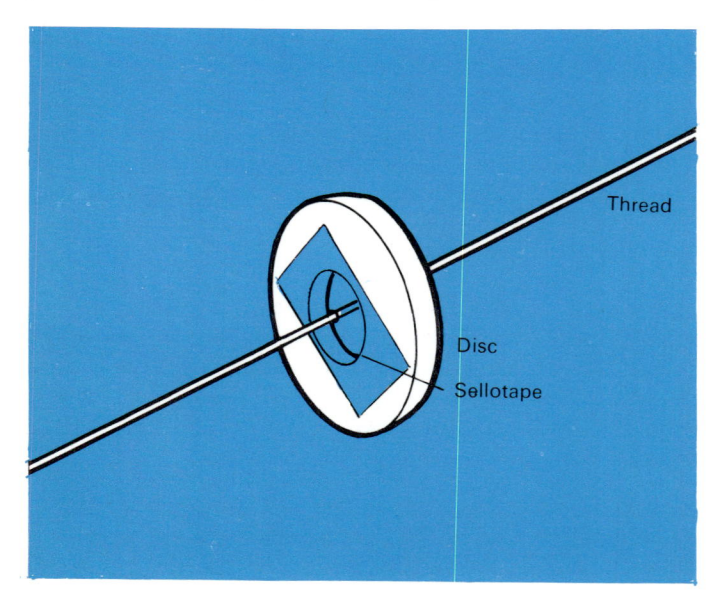

The following results were gained by testing in this way.

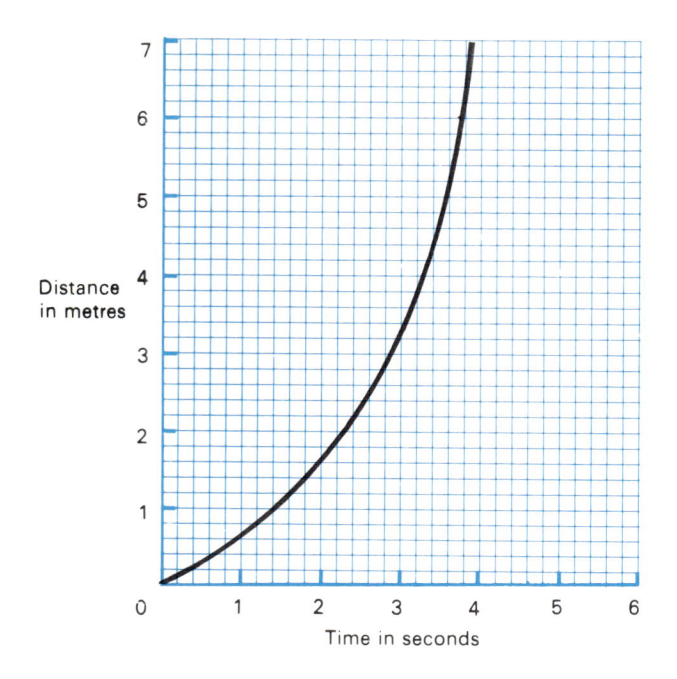

Distances travelled	2 metres	4 metres	6 metres
Time of 1st run(s)	3	3·75*	3·5
Time of 2nd run(s)	2	3	4
Time of 3rd run(s)	2	3	3·75
Average time(s)	2·3	3·25	3·75

* Slowed by wind resistance.

A second method involves interrupting the slider's journeys at increasing intervals of time and measuring the distances it has covered. If the children give the slider some trial runs before testing they can get a good idea of the distances it is likely to travel in two, four, and six seconds and position somebody in readiness to catch it. A child observing the seconds timer can give another member of the group the signals to release and stop the slider.

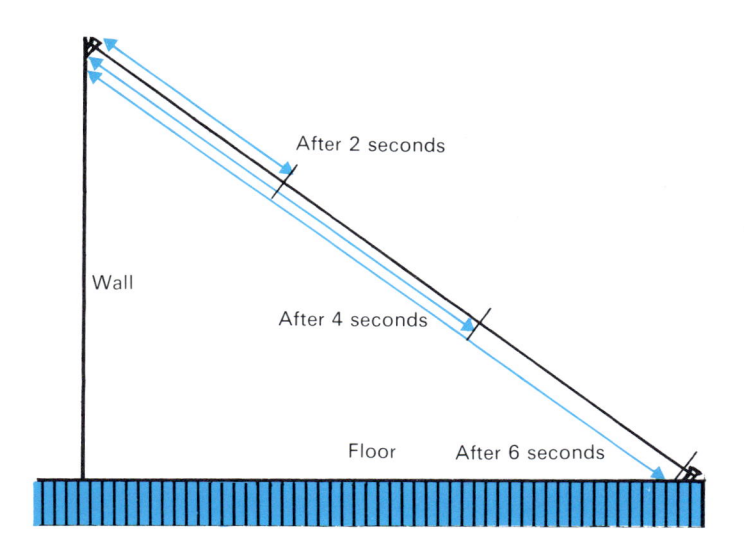

From this type of result children can see that the distances covered are increasing to a greater extent than the times allowed for the journeys. This could only happen if the slider is gaining speed.

Through this kind of experience children could begin to build up ideas about *acceleration.* However, it should be emphasised that at this stage it is sufficient for children to establish the fact that speed does increase. More precise investigations into ideas about acceleration will not be appropriate until two or three years later, for example see Nuffield *O-Level Physics Teacher's Guide 3,* page 232 and *Guide to Experiments 3,* pages 174-90, (Longman & Penguin).

Beginning with a seesaw

Children who have enjoyed using the seesaw can be encouraged to think about the way it can be affected by different pairs of children.

Which children always make one end move downwards?
Which children can keep the seat level when they sit in similar places?
Which children can keep the seat level by sitting in different places?
Can a small light child find a way of raising a heavy child?

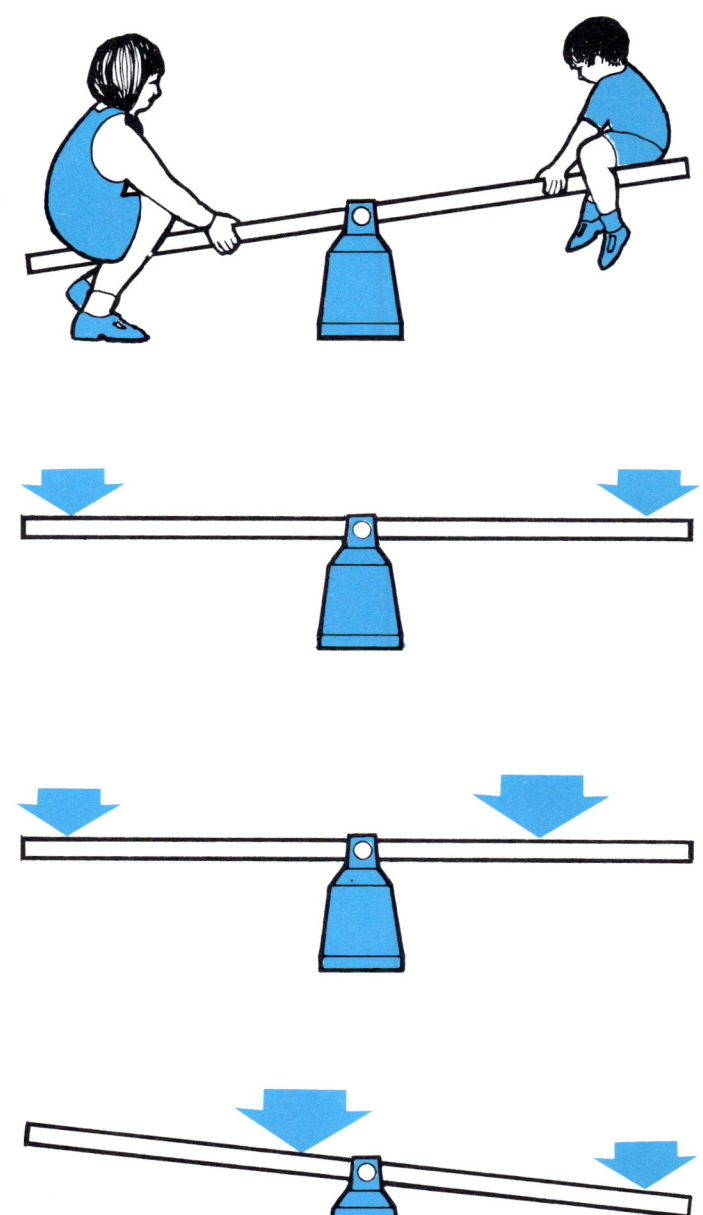

Here they are really playing with a lever which is a bar arranged so that it can be turned about a point or pivot. Fulcrum is another name for the pivot. This arrangement

75

can be varied in many ways. This is something children find interesting when they collect examples of the many ways levers are used in everyday life.

They could begin with pieces of Meccano. Where can we put the turning point?

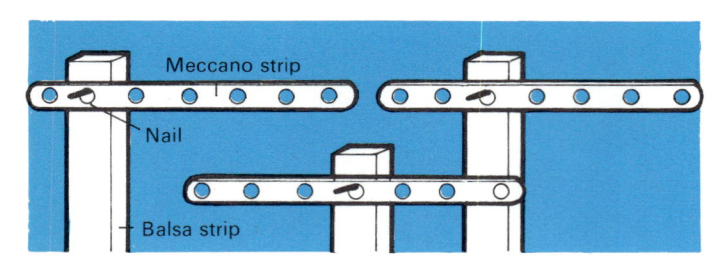

Where are the turning points in these lever arrangements?

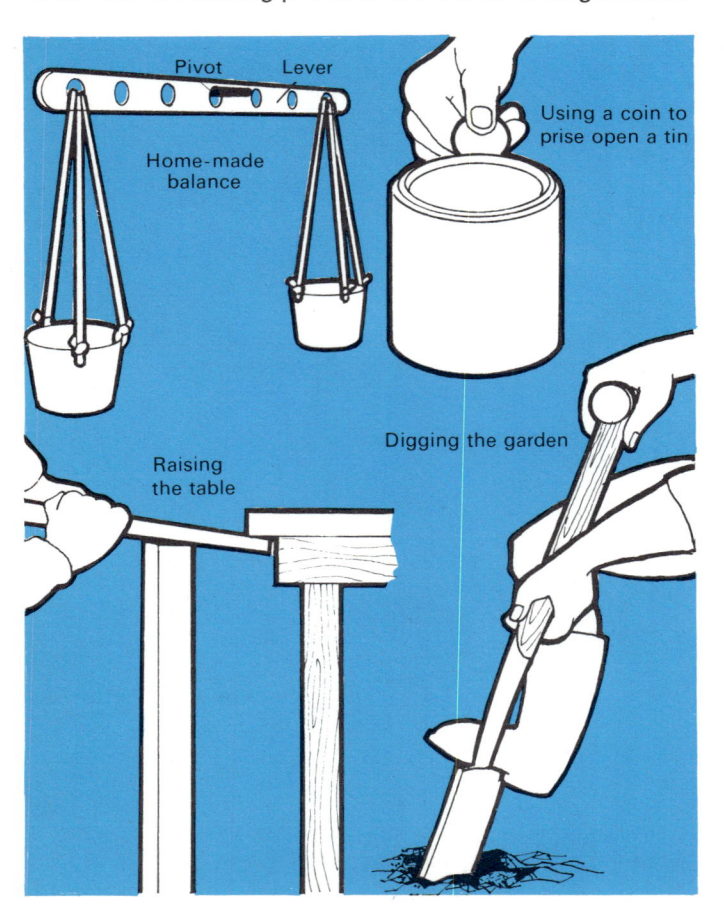

In what positions can we have the bar?

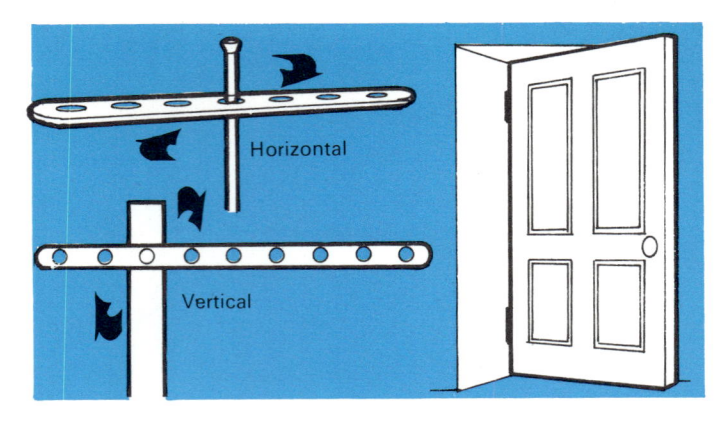

The size and shape of the bar can vary too.

Can we have two bars turning about the same pivot?

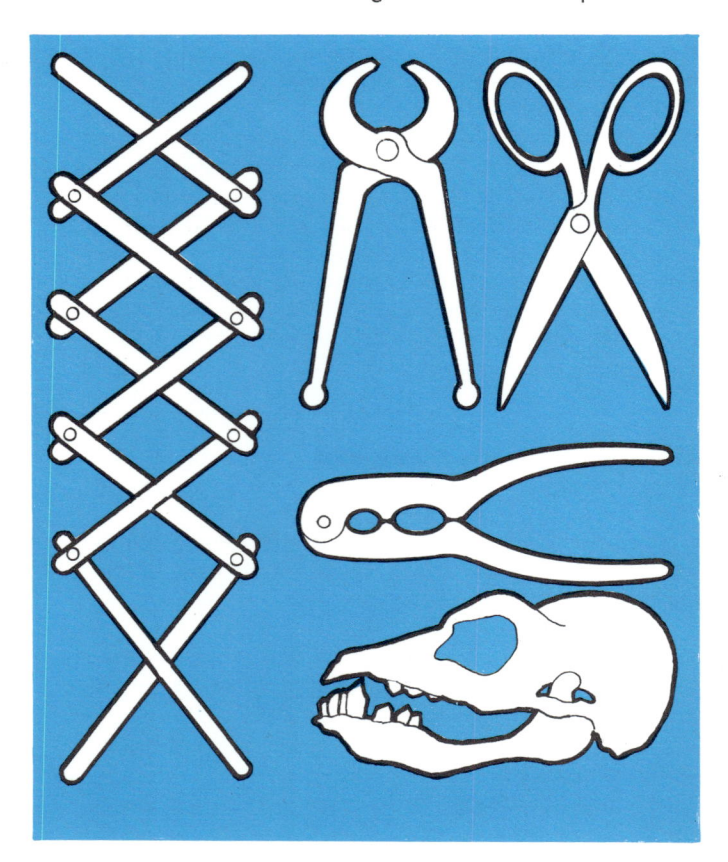

How far do different parts of the bar move when it turns?

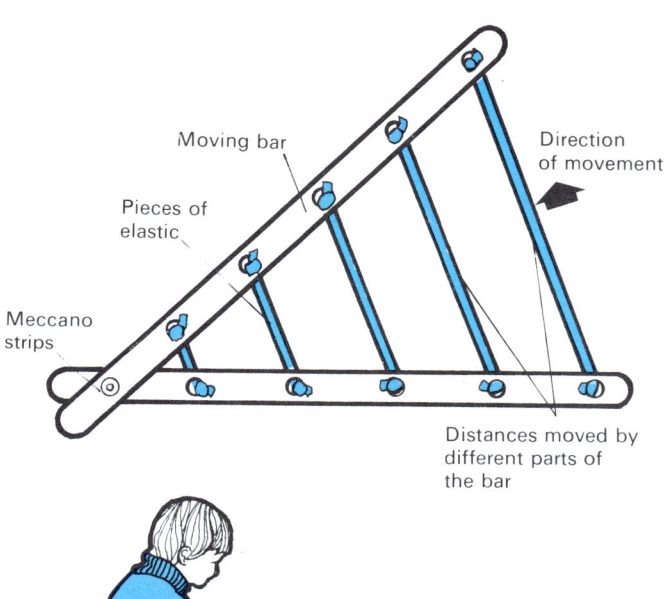

How can a lever be used to magnify the growth of a plant? (See page 29.)

Pushes and pulls are required to make the lever turn. Where on the bar are they most effective?

Try opening the gate by pulling in different places.

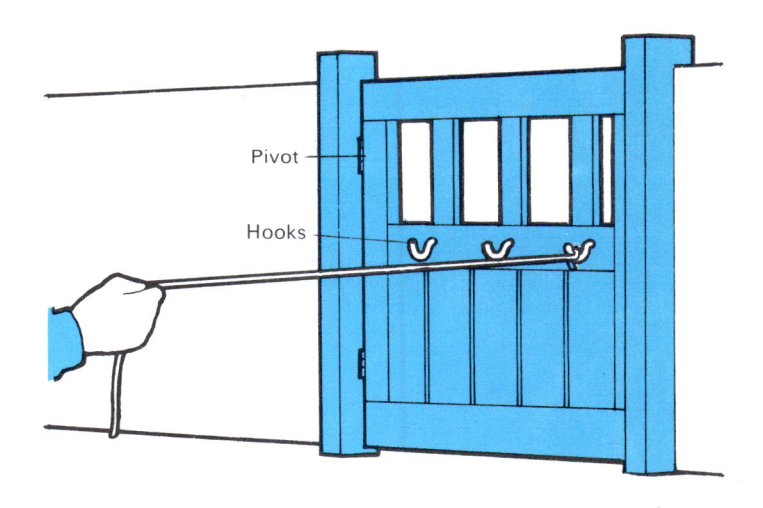

Where is the best place for a door handle?

How can the smallest boy lift the heavy bucket?

77

This is the kind of experience that can help children to grasp the idea of the distance from the pivot where the force (push or pull) is applied, which makes a considerable difference to its effectiveness.

Now a mathematical equaliser can be useful. Children can use it to find out more about the relationship between force (F) and distance (D) in bringing about the turning effect on the bar of a lever.

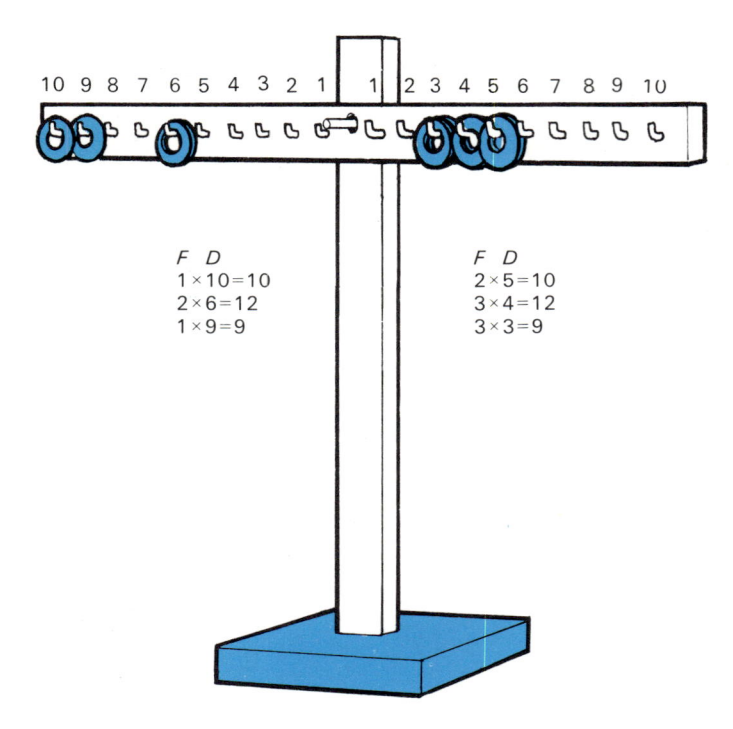

10 9 8 7 6 5 4 3 2 1   1 2 3 4 5 6 7 8 9 10

F	D			F	D	
1 × 10	= 10			2 × 5	= 10	
2 × 6	= 12			3 × 4	= 12	
1 × 9	= 9			3 × 3	= 9	

In the figure above the gravitational pulls on the washers provide the force (F) to turn the bar. The place where they are hung gives the distance from the pivot (D). $F \times D$ gives the turning effect.

When children try to balance the bar they are trying to balance the turning effects they create on each side. Although the number of washers and their positions on each side of the bar may differ, their product ($F \times D$) must be the same on each side if the bar is to be balanced. This was what the children tried to do with their own bodies when they tried to balance themselves on the seesaw in the park.

Beginning with a swing

Swings can serve as good starting points for work with pendulums, because when a child seated on a swing is drawn backward and then released he is in the same situation as the bob of a pendulum. He can experience the regularity of the to and fro movement involved, think of the pathway along which his body moves (an arc ⌒) and consider what could be counted as a complete swing or oscillation.

Pendulums

These provide a rewarding topic for further investigation in school. So many things connected with them can be varied, and the effects can be measured.

Here are some suggestions for variations.

1. The bob's mass size, shape and the material of which it is made.

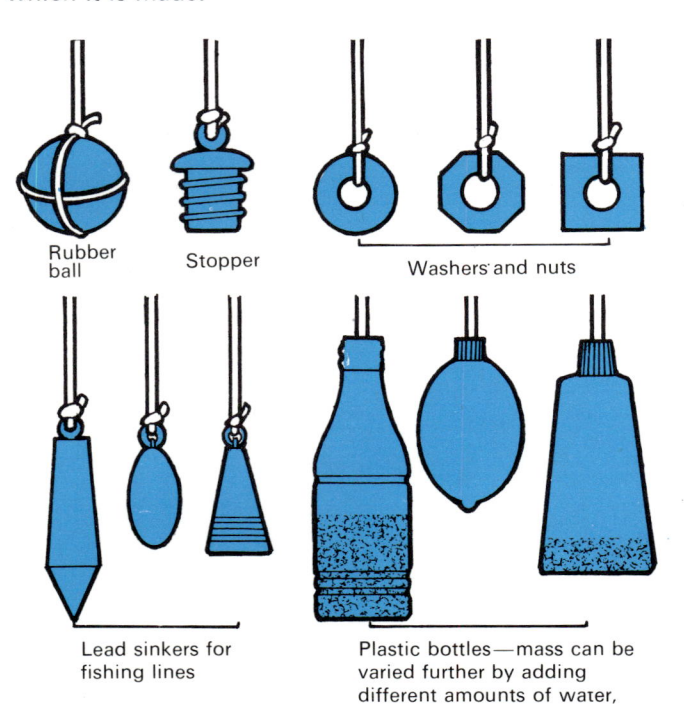

Rubber ball   Stopper   Washers and nuts

Lead sinkers for fishing lines

Plastic bottles—mass can be varied further by adding different amounts of water, salt, or fine silver sand

2. The length of the pendulum.
The length is taken as the measurement from the point of attachment to the centre of gravity of the bob.

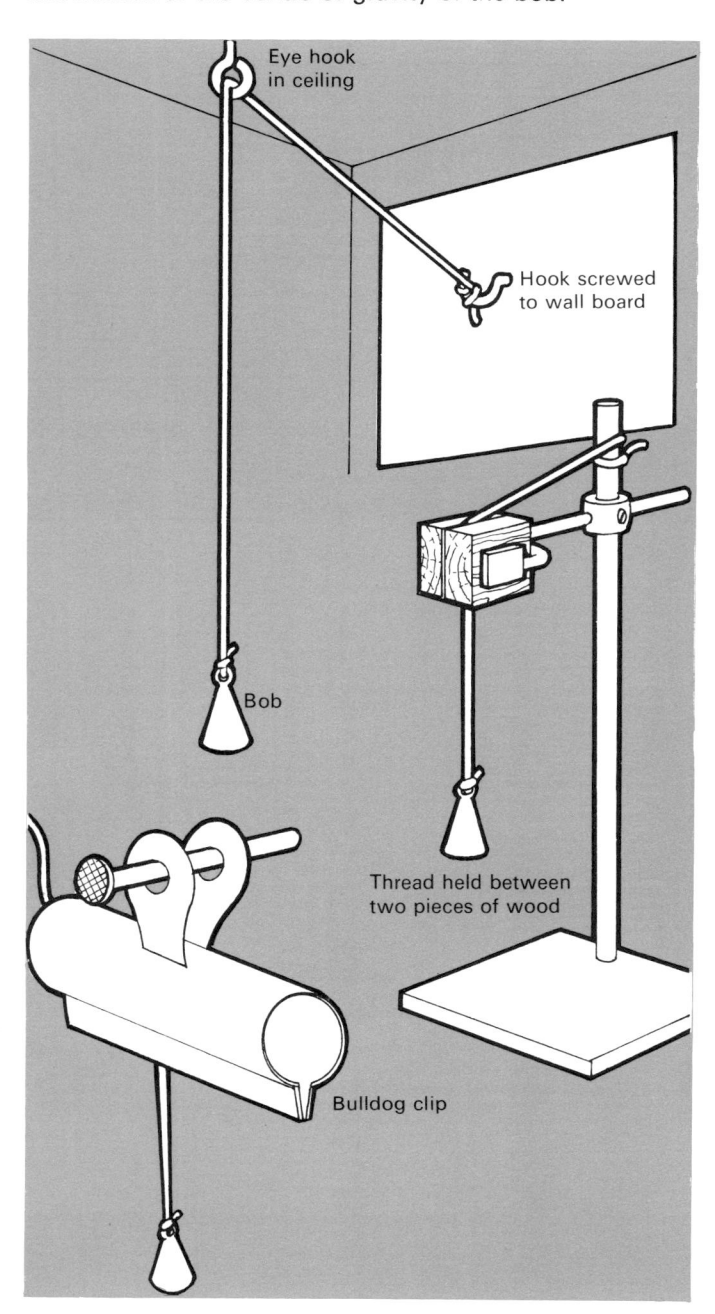

3. The position of the pendulum.
Interesting tests can be conducted by arranging pendulums in different ways.

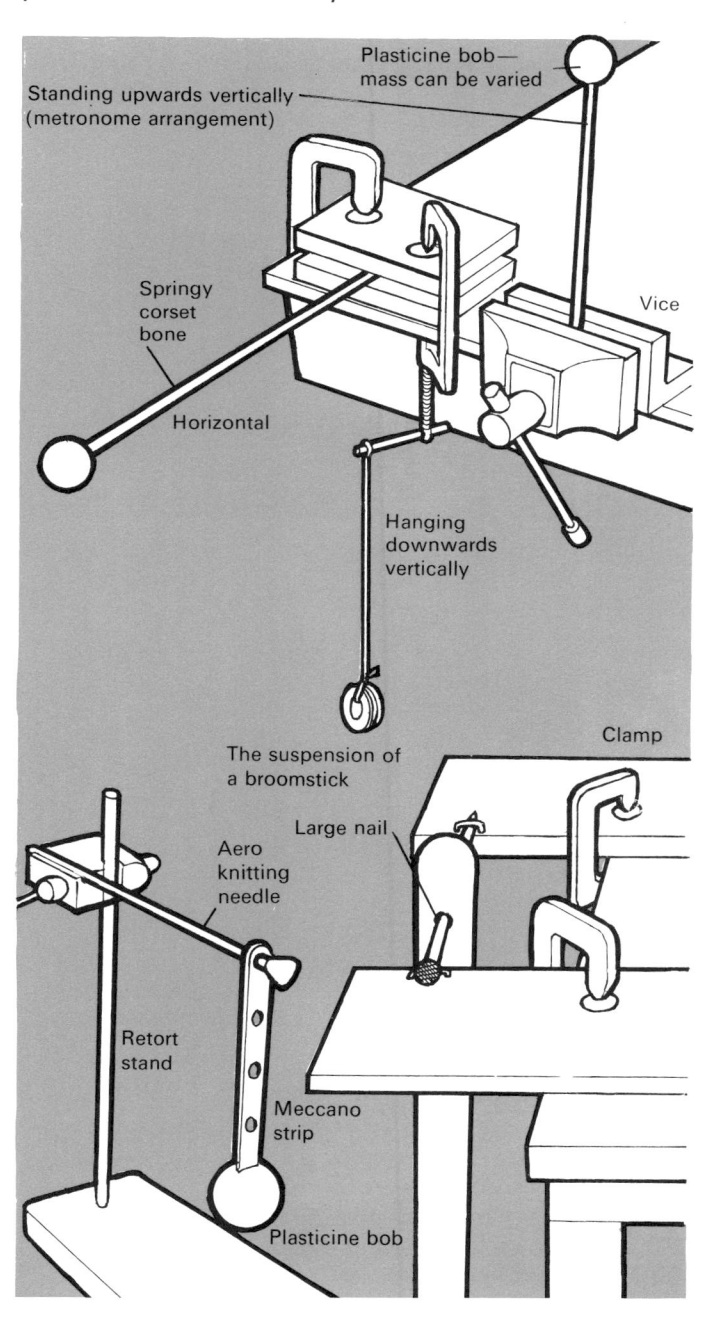

79

4. The following materials could be used for suspending the bob.

String, tape, nylon monofilament (fishing line).
Circular elastic, knicker elastic, catapult elastic, a spring, all of which stretch and contract.
Strips of metal or plastic Meccano, Bilofix, a broomstick, which are rigid.
A corset bone, which is springy.

Set the pendulum in motion by raising the bob until its thread forms an angle of about 45° with the vertical position and then release it. Each to and fro swing takes the same length of time. Galileo used this fact in his work on clocks.

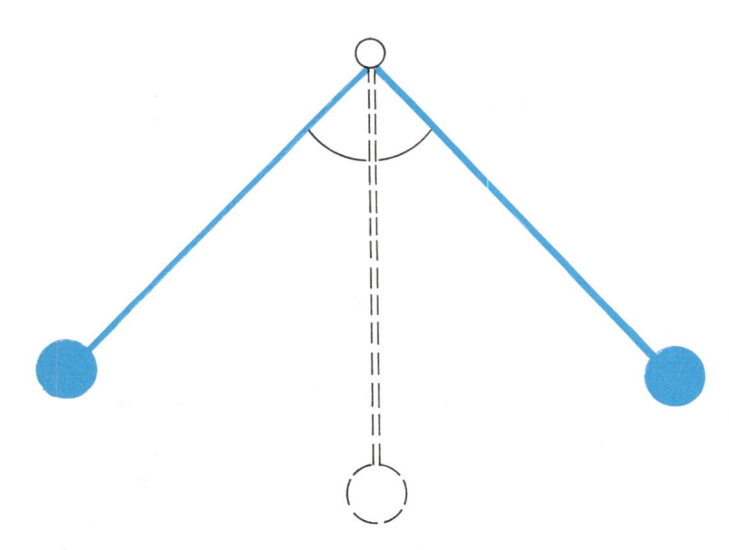

Now children can try to discover which of all the variations possible cause a pendulum to swing faster or more slowly. They can also tackle the problem of setting up pendulums that take given periods of time to make each complete swing.

The best way of encouraging children to think of their own ways of doing these things is to provide them with a wide assortment of materials for bobs and threads and different devices for fixing them in position. Scissors for effecting alterations and seconds timers are also useful. When their own ideas give out they will need the help of the teacher's questions.

Some children may like to produce a ticking device or they could try to gain further information by observing a sand pendulum.

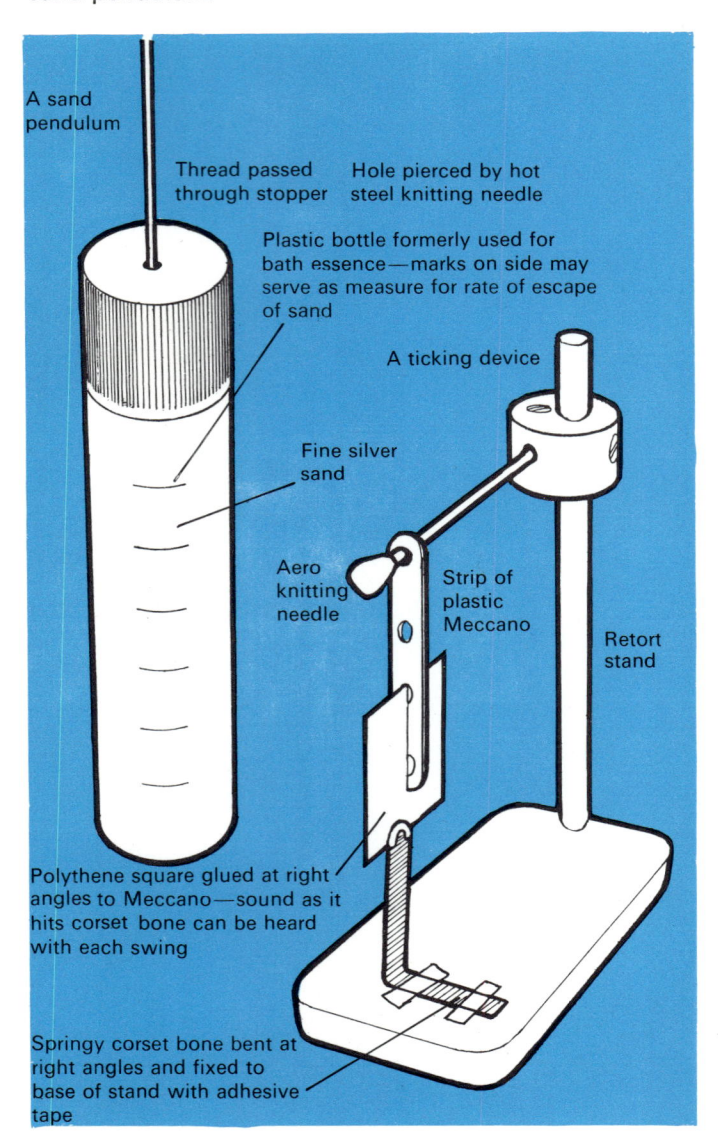

A sand pendulum
- Thread passed through stopper
- Hole pierced by hot steel knitting needle
- Plastic bottle formerly used for bath essence—marks on side may serve as measure for rate of escape of sand
- A ticking device
- Fine silver sand
- Aero knitting needle
- Strip of plastic Meccano
- Retort stand
- Polythene square glued at right angles to Meccano—sound as it hits corset bone can be heard with each swing
- Springy corset bone bent at right angles and fixed to base of stand with adhesive tape

For many further ideas for investigation with pendulums see *Time,* Science 5/13, pages 21–28 (Macdonald Educational, 1972), and J. W. Bainbridge, R. W. Stockdale and E. R. Wastnedge *Junior Science Source Book,* pages 139–43 (Collins, 1970).

Beginning on things that go round

What does it feel like to go round and round quickly?
Why is it necessary to hold on tightly?
What about trying to make a model that spins things round like the roundabout at the fair?
What happens to the seats when it is set going?
What prevents the seats getting away from the model?

What can get away when a wet sponge is swung round and round?
Could this idea be used for making a spin drier?
There are some good suggestions in the Unit *Holes, gaps and cavities* (pages 63-64).

There are many other ways in which materials are swung round and round to be mixed. Have a good look at the food mixer in action or the cement mixer on the building site.
What prevents the materials being mixed from flying away?

Children who become interested in circular movements of different things would enjoy making use of the book *Moving Round and Round* by A. James (Schofield & Sims, 1963). It contains many suggestions about things to do.

Making a model roundabout

5 Work with birds

Although concrete, smoke and traffic have driven many living things from towns, certain birds have become well adapted to urban conditions. Birds can be seen in towns in the streets or sitting high up on the ledges of buildings. In residential areas they are to be found in gardens or nesting in the eaves of houses; they use television aerials as song perches. In the parks they will delight children by their antics and they will scavenge the town corporation dumps.

Many children become keenly interested in birds. However, too often they try to find out more about them only by collecting pictures and copying from reference books, instead of using their own eyes and ears. Perhaps the following ideas will help teachers who wish to help children to become genuine bird-watchers.

Recognition

This ability will develop gradually. Plenty of help and information must be provided.

First of all, birds should be attracted to places where they may be watched by supplies of food and shallow water (see Volume 4, pages 29–30). Thus their names may be gradually learned. Sharp movements will startle birds and make them take flight. Children should separate for watching, and try to find ways of making themselves inconspicuous.

Older children between the ages of ten and thirteen may like to construct a hide if they can find a good place in the school grounds. This can be particularly useful for watching birds in their natural nesting sites or boxes they have occupied; or for photography.*

A pair of binoculars (8×30) can be a great stimulus to observation. Helpful advice about choosing them is given in J. Taunton, *Bird Projects for Schools* (Evans, 1969).

---

*See also Ennion, E. A. R., Bird Study in a Garden, *Puffin Picture Book, page 27.* Campbell, B., Bird Watching for Beginners, *Puffin Story Book, page 194 (Penguin, 1952).*

Enlarged views of timid birds keeping their distance can be obtained with the help of a telescope. Children aged ten or more may like to make their own. For this a pair of suitable convex lenses is required, namely one with a short focal length (5 cm (2 in) approx.) and one with a long focal length (25·5 cm (10 in) approx.).

Test different arrangements to find the combination that brings the view of an object nearer and the right way up at the same time. When this has been discovered, the lenses can be fixed in an adjustable holder by following directions for making a telescope given by A. James in *Simple Science Experiments* (Schofield & Sims, 1964).

Outlines of birds with labels indicating the main areas of the body can be duplicated.

Children can colour in the different parts and then try to match their completed pictures with illustrations in books of identification.

Children could also be encouraged to make rapid sketches of birds in different positions.

Illustrations for matching
Accurately coloured pictures should be made available for matching with things seen.

Postcards can be obtained from the British Museum of Natural History, Cromwell Road, London SW7, as well as from stationers and booksellers. Those published by J. Arthur Dixon Ltd, of Newport, Isle of Wight, are particularly good.

Charts can be bought from the Royal Society for the Protection of Birds, The Lodge, Sandy, Bedfordshire. Coloured transparencies and film strips can be obtained from: Diana Wyllie Ltd, 3 Park Road, London NW1; Educational Productions Ltd, East Ardsley, Wakefield, Yorkshire, or 27–28 Maunsel Street, London SW1.

The following information was collected by a group of six-year-old children in an urban school.

Counting birds

A single count will show little or nothing, but when the numbers of birds seen in certain places are noted regularly over longer periods, more representative records will emerge and it may be possible to make some interesting comparisons.

Note that the numbers compiled by children will always be approximate, since without ringing, a technique requiring special training and skill, it is impossible to be certain that the same bird has not been counted twice.

Children may discover through their regular recordings that some birds can be seen at all seasons and others only at certain times of the year. This will be a good moment to discuss migration.

Things we have found out by watching the birds on our bird table		
How birds move	**Bird behaviour**	**Bird colours**
Starlings waddle	Sparrows are frightened of seagulls	Blue tits—blue yellow green white black
Sparrows hop	Starlings are greedy	
Seagulls swoop	Sparrows have to flap their wings when they hang on the bacon rind but blue tits do not have to flap their wings	Sparrows—brown grey white black
Starlings can balance on the string		Starlings—green purple black white
Starlings run		It shines very brightly in the sun
Seagulls can land on a small surface when they want food	Seagulls are greedy	Coal tits—black yellow grey brown
	Only the blue tit came to the coconut	Seagulls—white grey black
Seagulls glide		Thrushes—white grey black fawn
Blue tits flap their wings ever so fast	Two blackbirds visited our bird table	The male blackbird is a much nicer colour than the female. The male is a shiny black, the female is a dull brown

Observing one type of bird

A number of the same type of bird may collect in certain places in built-up areas, for instance:

Seagulls on a school field.
Mallard ducks on a park lake.
Pigeons in a street or market place.
Wood pigeons in a park.
Sparrows in a street.
Blackbirds seen from different viewing points in the grounds of a school.

A daily count of individuals in this type of collection can be made at the same time each day to see whether numbers vary, and whether there is any pattern in the variation.

Such a study can be undertaken while children's ability to recognise many birds is still uncertain.

Possible fluctuations in numbers at different times throughout the day can also be investigated.

Differences within a group

As children continue their observations they may find interesting differences in members of the population they are studying.

Do daily counts reveal any alteration in the numbers of the different types in relation to the whole population?

Counting different species of birds

David Mitchell, aged thirteen, was a member of the Limehurst Natural History Society in Loughborough. While on his paper-round in the Shelthorpe district of Loughborough he recorded the numbers of different birds he saw each morning between 8.00 and 8.45 am, from 3 December to 6 February. He found that certain birds were present in the bird population in greater numbers than others. Some graphs of his results are illustrated on the next page, and they could give rise to many interesting discussions.

Comparatively few blackbirds and thrushes were recorded, yet such birds are usually very common. Were there more in gardens and parks than in the streets where David made his counts?

Numbers of birds were higher on certain days. Is there any connection between the comings and goings of birds and differences in weather conditions? Children regularly keeping weather records could tackle this question. At times the seagull count was high, yet Loughborough is far from the coast. Were these birds driven inland by bad weather?

It would be interesting to make similar observations during the months from April to September, to discover whether summer migrants could be recorded.

A cuckoo might well be heard on a morning paper round.

Examples	Differences	
Pigeons vary in colour	Dark and light grey, whitish and light brown	
A group of seagulls may contain both herring, common and black-headed species	Herring gull	Large, light grey back and wings, black on wing tips, flesh coloured legs
	Common gull	Smaller than herring gull, similar colouring of feathers, greenish yellow legs and beak
	Black-headed gull	Similar in size to common gull, black head in summer only, white edge to wings, red bill and legs
Mallard ducks	Male	Green head, body white, brown and black. Distinctive colours lost in summer when it is darker brown than mate
	Female	Dullish brown, blue feathers in wing tips
Blackbirds	Male	Black, yellow beak
	Female	Dark brown

85

Crows

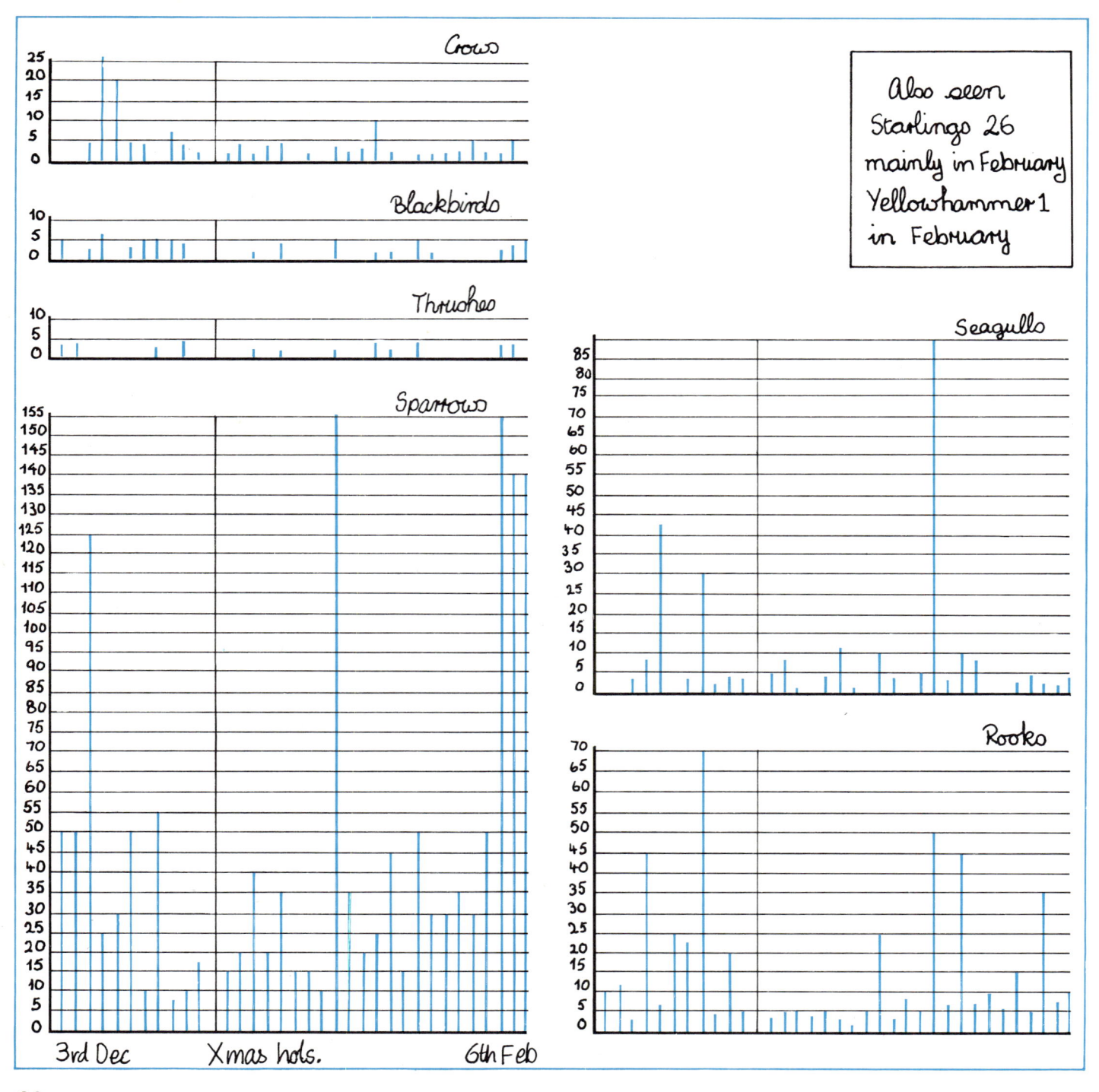

Blackbirds

Thrushes

Sparrows

Seagulls

Rooks

Also seen
Starlings 26
mainly in February
Yellowhammer 1
in February

3rd Dec — Xmas hols. — 6th Feb

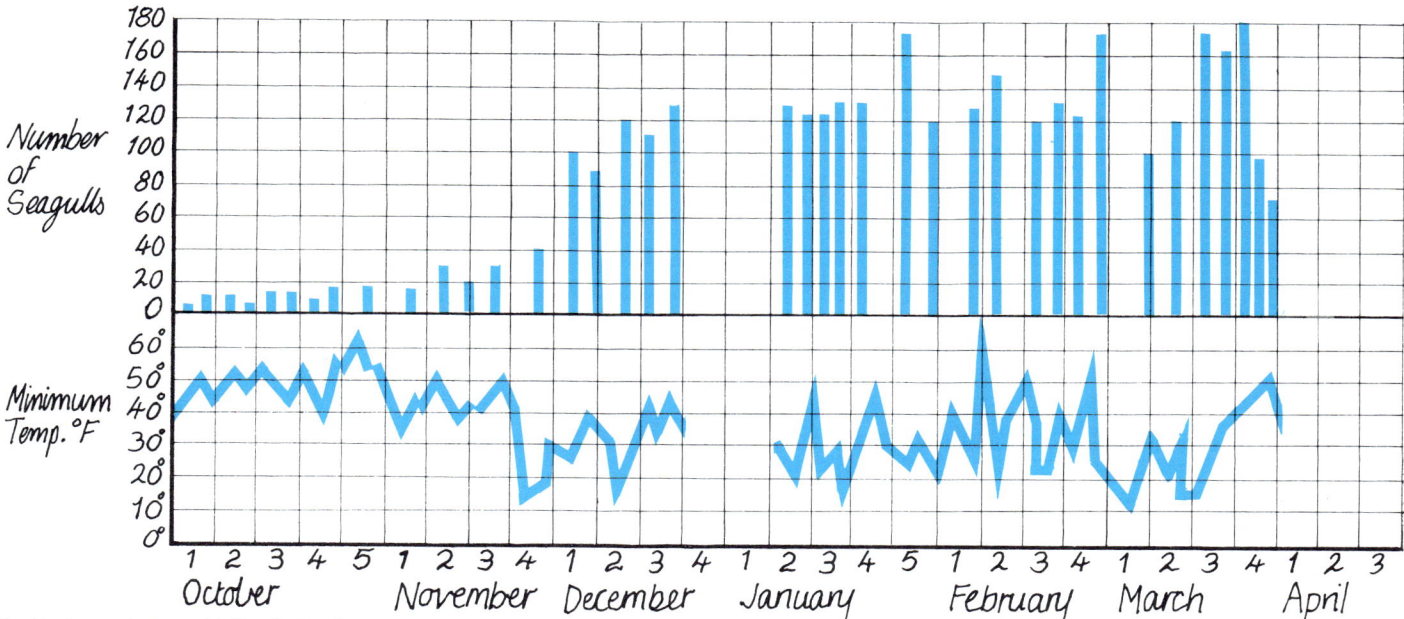

By kind permission of Miss B. Bayliss

A bird census and temperature
As part of their general studies course, girls from the sixth form of Ilford County High School counted black-headed gulls visiting a selected area of Valentine's Park which is adjacent to their school grounds, from October to April of the following year. Temperature records were kept at the same time. Above is a copy of their records, which suggest a correlation between temperature and the number of gulls, since more visited the district in cold weather.

Is there a relationship between wind direction and bird numbers?
A bird census can be combined with records of wind direction on a wind rose as shown on the right.

Use map pins of one colour to represent single birds counted, such as starlings, and map pins of another colour to represent five of the same bird.

Take the wind direction and on each occasion fill in an appropriate square on the wind rose. Then make a count of the birds in a selected area and add the correct number of map pins.

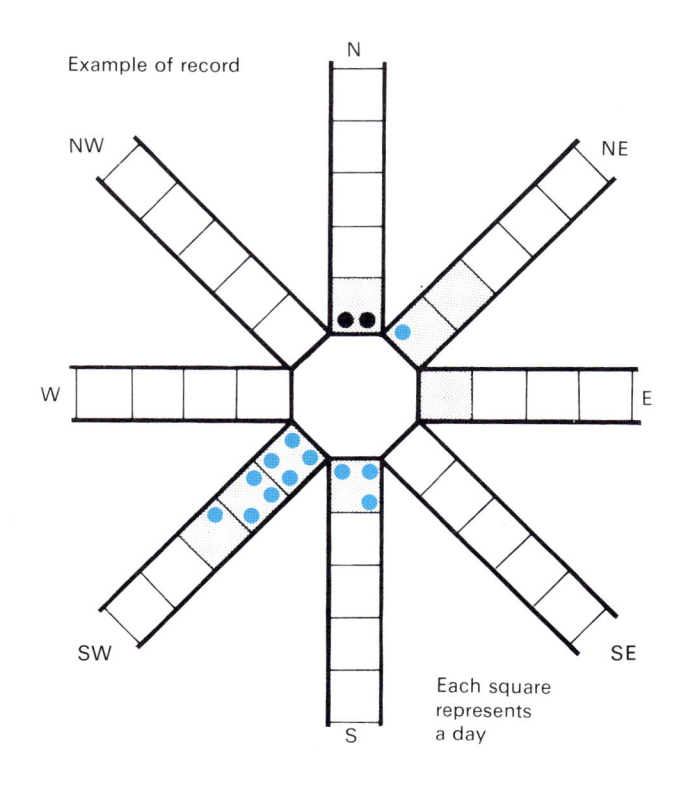

Example of record

Each square represents a day

A class study of the distribution of some common birds

Children can be encouraged to extend their observations beyond the school premises and school hours in the following way.

At the beginning of term supply a few large-scale base maps (1 : 1250 [50·680 in to 1 mile]) of an area such as a housing estate around the school and some boxes of coloured map pins to represent a few of the birds with which children are most familiar.

Encourage children to maintain a lookout for these birds and record their positions by placing pins in the appropriate places on the maps.

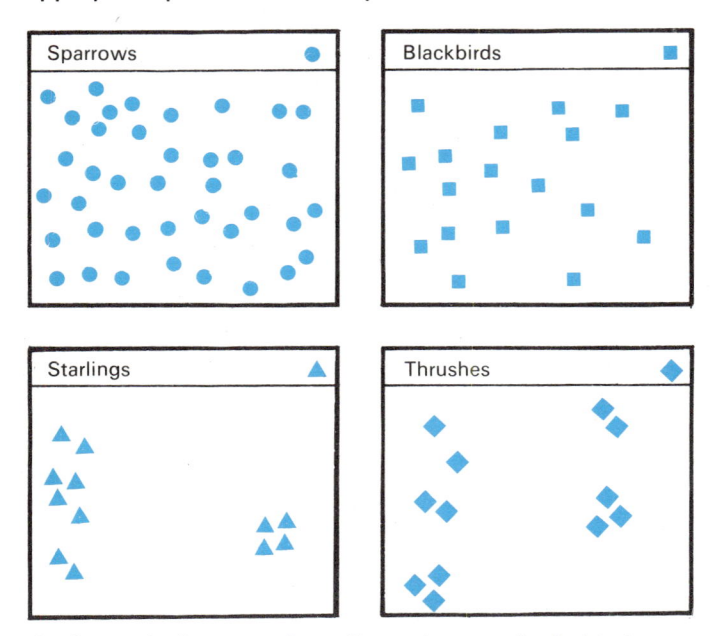

At the end of term a class discussion can be held about these records. Here are some of the questions about the birds that can be posed:

Which are most common?
Which have only been seen in gardens?
Which will stand on roads and pathways?
Which appear to be less timid when people are about?
Which perch on high things such as chimney stacks and television aerials and sing?
Which only appear where nuts are provided?

Visitors to bird tables

When children try to keep records of the birds which visit their bird tables and the birds that feed from the ground they will be concerned with a larger number of different birds at the same time.

In one infant school situated near a busy main road in Maidstone the six- to seven-year-old children recorded the birds on and around the bird table near their classroom window by placing ticks against names listed on a class chart. This interested Neil very much, so he followed up this work with his own survey made at home and the next morning presented his teacher with a little chart containing his results. Encouraged by her appreciation he spent some time in school that morning writing an account of his efforts.

Playground bird records

Older children can use duplicated check lists for more precise investigations of all the birds visiting an area of the school grounds during the same fifteen-minute period each day.

Viewing point: Date: Time of daily observation: Weather: Wind direction: Cloud cover:										Total
Sparrow	✓	✓	✓	✓	✓	✓	✓	✓	✓	10
Thrush	✓	✓								2
Blackbird	✓	✓	✓	✓	✓					5
Robin	–									–
Starling	✓	✓	✓							3
Wren	–									–
Blue tit	✓	✓								2
Bullfinch	✓									1

Neil's bird survey.

	Wed	Thurs	Fri	Sat	Sun
Thrushes	✓✓	✓✓	✓✓✓	✓✓	✓✓
Starlings	✓	✓✓	✓✓✓✓	✓✓✓	✓✓
Sparrows	✓✓✓✓	✓✓✓✓	✓✓✓✓✓	✓✓✓	✓✓✓
Tits					
Robins	✓✓	✓		✓	
Blackbirds	✓✓✓✓	✓✓	✓✓✓	✓✓	✓✓✓

We put the days of the week and we put some nams of the birds and we put some ticks in each colm we just put out bread and we stod in the kitchen and watched and counted the birds

---

The information should be inserted on the first section of the sheet before observations of birds are recorded.

At the end of a week daily counts can be combined on a block diagram which can be collected in a book of records ready for further study.

The same colours should be used on all the block diagrams for indicating the same birds.

If the school grounds are sufficiently large and contain various habitats such as field, rough ground, shrubs and trees, rockery, etc, this work could be extended to compare the birds using these different places during the same periods of time.

Why are there no birds?
Sometimes children and teachers become discouraged because no birds appear even when food and nesting materials are provided and the observers are well concealed.

A few years ago some teachers attending a course of in-service training decided to try to record the birds frequenting a strip of woodland on the edge of Wimbledon Common adjacent to a busy road at different times each day. When they said that they wished to abandon their study, they were challenged to try to discover why no birds had appeared.

When they looked more closely at the strip of woodland they were able to suggest the following reasons for the absence of bird life there:

There were no supplies of natural food.
It was near a busy main road, so the risk of noise and disturbance was great.
Too many children from an adjacent block of flats used the strip as a play area.
The belt of trees was too narrow.

These reasons were tested in the following ways.

The area was carefully searched for food supplies: insects, berries and seeds. Only a few insects and sycamore and maple seeds were discovered. The soil was acid and therefore unlikely to contain many worms.

The area and a comparable strip of woodland in a College of Education on the opposite side of the road were observed for the same length of time each day for birds and human beings. In both areas noise from traffic was similar but children and adults came frequently only to the area on the common. Garden birds were recorded on the other strip.

On the common there were also equally narrow belts of trees further from the main road where birds were seen.

The strip on the edge of the common was observed on several occasions at an early hour (5.00–6.00 am) when the presence of some birds was noted. Birds were also seen flying right over the area.

This study was carried out in August when birds sing less and do not collect food and nesting materials as vigorously as during the spring months. Different results might have been obtained in winter or spring.

There was, however, some evidence that lack of suitable food and frequent disturbance by human beings might be limiting bird life.

It is important to emphasise the fact that negative results in preliminary investigations can provide problems worth tackling. This type of work should not be offered to children too soon. It might appeal to children of twelve or thirteen years of good ability, but younger children are more likely to be interested in working on problems in which results are more positive.

The value of long-term studies

Long-term quantitative studies can only be successful when organisation is good and observers dependable. They are therefore more suitable for older children. They show children that regular routine work is often necessary if reliable evidence is to be obtained.

If records extending over a number of years can be accumulated, and these should have a place in a school resources area, they can be carefully examined to see whether phenomena like a particularly cold winter, mild weather in early spring, or a summer drought, seem to exert any influence on bird numbers and habits.

Such records would be worth exchanging with schools in other parts of the country or sending to the Biological Records Centre of the Nature Conservancy at Monks Wood Experimental Station at Abbots Ripton, Hunts.

Feeding habits

Further studies of the feeding habits of birds will often arise naturally from work on bird tables.

There are a number of food containers on the market that can be hung out of doors. Some children might be interested in comparing their relative powers of attraction.

Place the same quantities of shelled peanuts in these containers and suspend in the same area at the same height.

Count or weigh these nuts at the end of each day.
Do birds make more use of containers from which the peanuts can be extracted most easily?
Do they go for shelled rather than unshelled peanuts when both are offered?

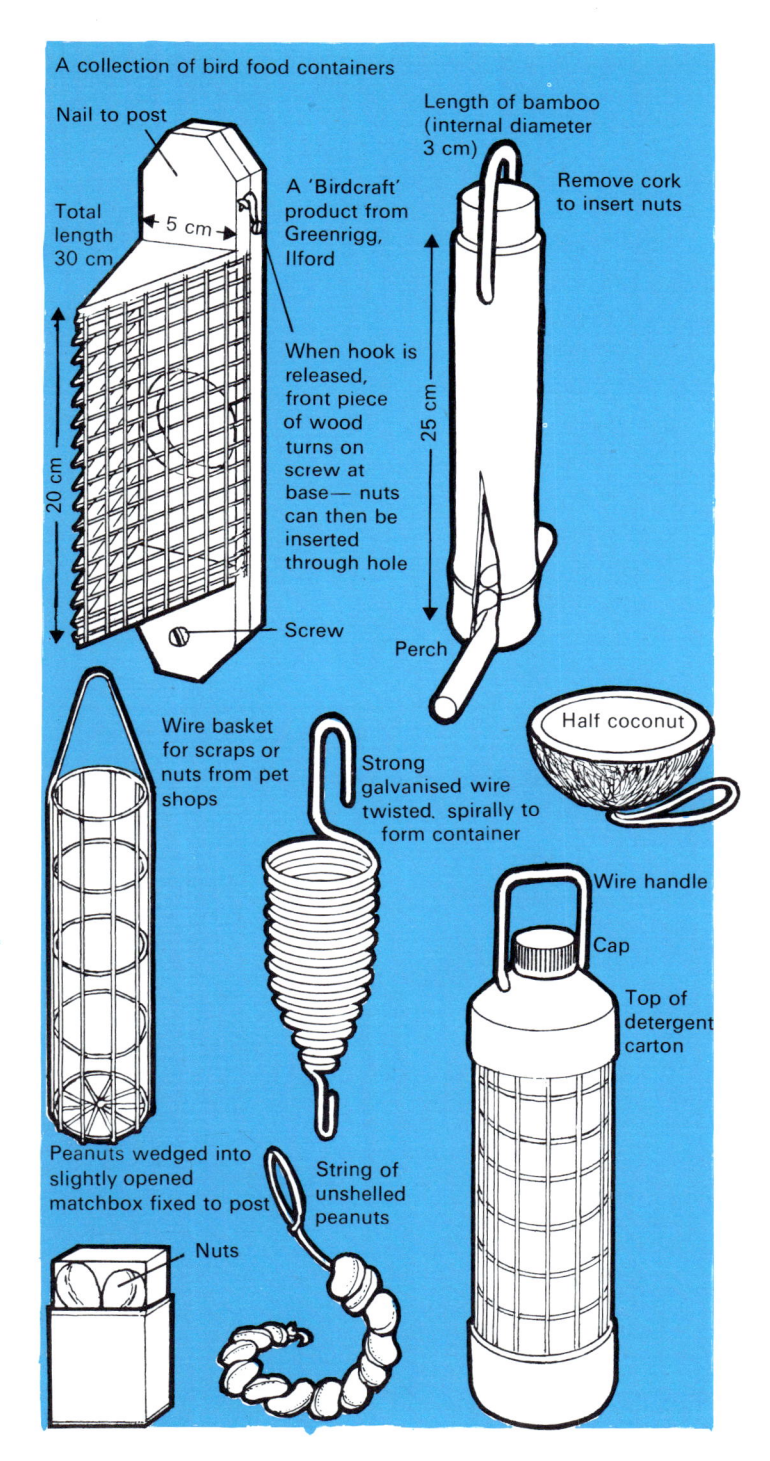

A collection of bird food containers

- Nail to post
- Total length 30 cm
- 5 cm
- 20 cm
- A 'Birdcraft' product from Greenrigg, Ilford
- When hook is released, front piece of wood turns on screw at base— nuts can then be inserted through hole
- Screw
- Length of bamboo (internal diameter 3 cm)
- Remove cork to insert nuts
- 25 cm
- Perch
- Wire basket for scraps or nuts from pet shops
- Strong galvanised wire twisted spirally to form container
- Half coconut
- Peanuts wedged into slightly opened matchbox fixed to post
- Nuts
- String of unshelled peanuts
- Wire handle
- Cap
- Top of detergent carton

Are different results obtained if these containers are placed on the ground instead of suspended?
Tits and greenfinches readily eat peanuts. Will they eat other materials as eagerly if nuts are not available?
Remove all nuts and suspend containers of other foodstuffs from the bird table or shrubs.

Do birds select particular things from the constituents of commercial wild bird food?
All members of the class can co-operate in making an analysis of the constituents of a packet of Swoop or Scramble. Show the results as a block diagram.

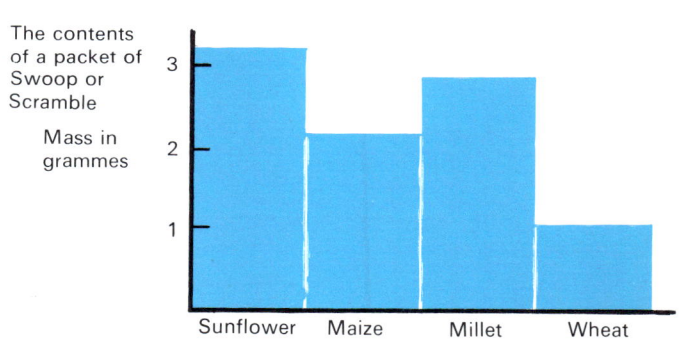

The contents of a packet of Swoop or Scramble
Mass in grammes

Sunflower   Maize   Millet   Wheat

When this has been done, the constituents can be mixed again and then divided between several shallow dishes. These can be placed on the bird table and the ground. Take them in at the end of the school day.

Make a block diagram of the constituents remaining, and compare them with the earlier graph.

Children will only obtain a very rough result because the birds tend to scatter the seeds around the dish while feeding. Some will germinate readily if they fall on suitable ground.

Further investigations on scattering seeds can be performed if a dish of Swoop is placed in the middle of an area of cleared ground 2 metres square. Regular weekly counts of any plants appearing on this patch can be made.

How many plants match the seeds originally found in the food mixture?
How many plants may have come from other sources?

Are some foods offered by human beings more attractive to birds than others?
In 1965, between 27 March and 9 April and from 25 April to 10 May, a class of ten- to eleven-year-old children each day placed weighed amounts of the following foods in dishes on the two bird tables and on the ground in the remains of an orchard covering a small part of their school grounds.

Orange peel	Apple
Raisins	Fat
Currants	Cereal
Eggshell	Bacon
Cooked potato	Rhubarb
Raw carrot	Scraps of bread
Cheese	

During these same periods their daily bird counts gave the results shown on the right.

Reweighing of the foodstuffs afterwards showed that most bacon and bread were eaten. Raisins, currants and cereal were next in popularity. Some cheese and fat were taken, and very small amounts of carrot and apple. Orange peel, egg shell, potato and rhubarb were ignored. Much more food was removed on sunny and dull days than on wet days.

Do tits take peanuts more readily from certain heights?
Hang six similar bags of shelled peanuts around one part of the school grounds, at different heights.

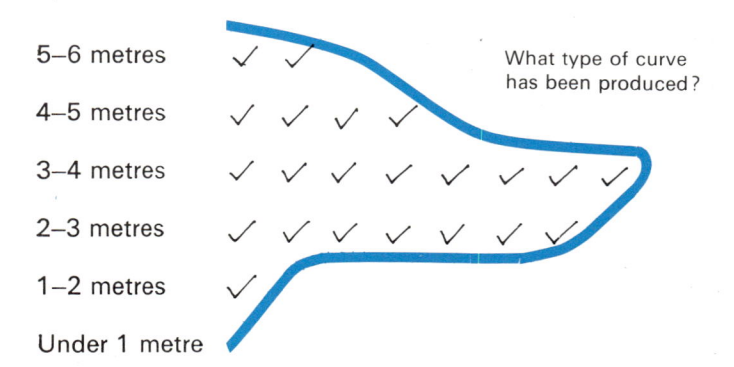

Height	Ticks
5–6 metres	✓ ✓
4–5 metres	✓ ✓ ✓ ✓
3–4 metres	✓ ✓ ✓ ✓ ✓ ✓ ✓
2–3 metres	✓ ✓ ✓ ✓ ✓ ✓
1–2 metres	✓
Under 1 metre	

What type of curve has been produced?

Record at hourly intervals throughout a school day the presence or absence of tits on the bags.

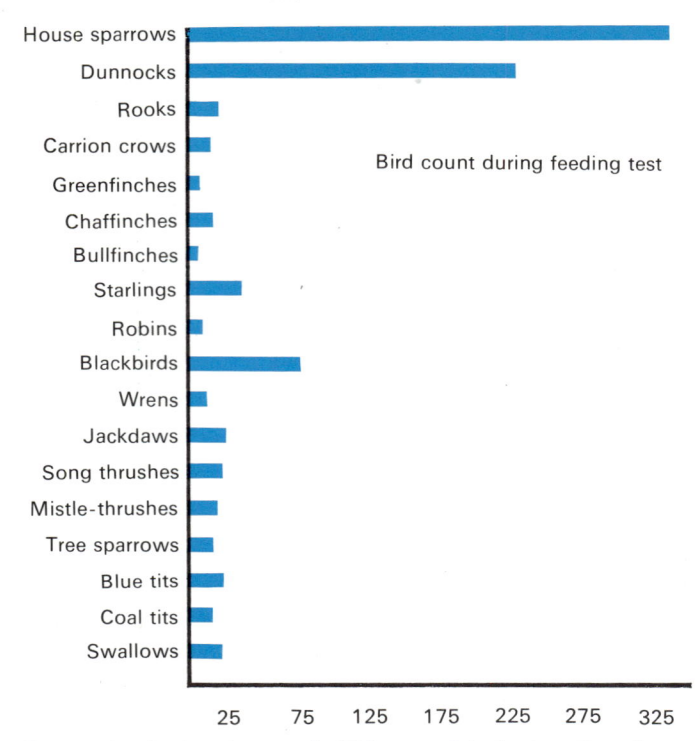

Bird count during feeding test

- House sparrows
- Dunnocks
- Rooks
- Carrion crows
- Greenfinches
- Chaffinches
- Bullfinches
- Starlings
- Robins
- Blackbirds
- Wrens
- Jackdaws
- Song thrushes
- Mistle-thrushes
- Tree sparrows
- Blue tits
- Coal tits
- Swallows

25 75 125 175 225 275 325

Does the behaviour of different birds feeding in the same area vary?
Which birds:

Feed from a bird table?
Feed from the ground?
Feed while hanging?
Show aggressive or greedy behaviour?
Are easily driven away from supplies?
Make further attempts to reach food when driven off?
Remove large portions?
Show no further interest when they drop food?
Feed continuously for some time?
Quickly move away from supplies?
Continue returning to the food supply until it is exhausted?
Make sounds whilst feeding?

Which birds:
Make most use of garden bird baths?
Do so in order to drink?
Do so for bathing?
Tolerate other birds in the water at the same time?

Characteristic movements

Try to observe one bird for ten minutes and record its movements and resting periods.

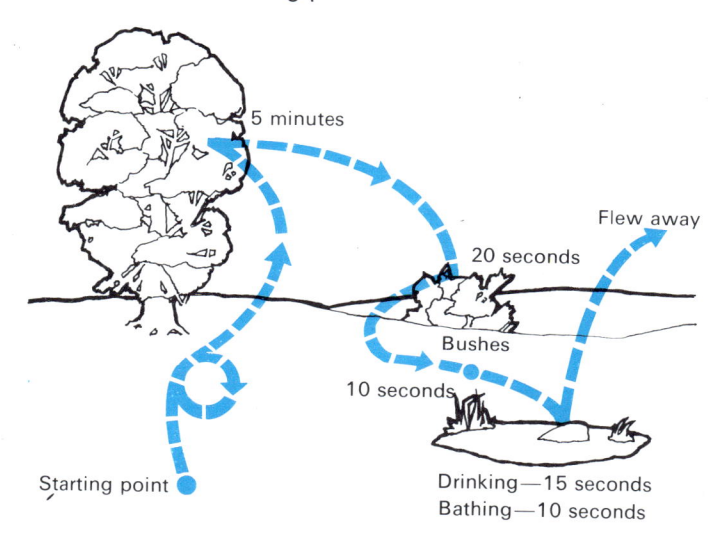

Try to collect information about bird deportment and behaviour.

1. Pose: does the bird hold its body upright, horizontally, or somewhere between the two?

2. Does it raise its tail when alighting on the ground or a fence, as blackbirds do?

3. What are its movements when not in flight, such as when bathing, either in water or in dust? How long does it take? What movements are involved?

4. What actions are involved when they preen their feathers?

5. Why do birds often fluff out their feathers in cold weather?

6. The feet of dead birds may be examined for features likely to help movement, such as webbing between the digits which gives a flat surface for pushing against water or walking on mud.

Flight

This is an extremely complex process. The wings and feathers change position all the time during flight. The muscular action is complicated. The air pressure on the upper and lower sides of the wings varies. Air currents are utilised.

Children below the age of thirteen are unlikely to be able to unravel the complete story. However, they can undertake some of the following investigations and so gain experience likely to contribute to fuller understanding at a later stage.

Flying movements

Encourage children to form the habit of watching birds flying. Do certain movements appear to be characteristic of certain birds? The following chart could be completed by relating birds' names to the types of movement that they are observed making while they are in the air.

Birds in flight		
Holding a straight course	Undulating (up and down)	Flapping
	Swallow	Pigeon
Gliding	Wheeling	Soaring
	Seagull Swallow	

Height and speed

Try to make the following estimations:

The height of birds in the air by comparison with a tree, house or television aerial whose height you have estimated (or measured).
The number of wing beats in a given period.
The speed at which birds move by finding out the time taken to fly between two landmarks fairly far apart. Note that strong winds retard speed, particularly at great heights. Calm days are best for these observations.

Wings
Shape

Is there any connection between wing shape and the type of flight?

Watch birds flying. Map pins can be used to record your observations on a chart. More information about the wing shapes of the birds you have seen in the air can be added to the chart subsequently from first-hand observation, the study of specimens in a museum or a class collection of wings, or reference books.

Name of bird	Type of flight	Skill in diving and turning	Wing Shape
Swallow	● (blue)	● (black)	○
Blackbird			
Thrush			
Sparrow			
Starling			

● Strong fliers   ○ Long narrow wings
■ Weak fliers (blue) ■ Short rounded wings (black)
● Skilful in diving and turning

A collection of wings and feathers from dead birds would be useful.

Sketch the silhouettes of some wings.

Black-headed gull   House sparrow

Where is the thickest part of the wing? In what position is it when the bird moves forward? It will be in front; hence this is called the leading edge. The trailing edge is the thin edge.

Feathers

In which part of the wing are:

The shortest feathers (coverts)?
The longest feathers (primary flight feathers)?
Medium-length feathers (secondary flight feathers)?
Carefully examine single feathers from different parts of the wing.
Examine a feather in detail and name its parts.
Sketches drawn to scale could show the proportions of the wing that the different types of feathers cover.

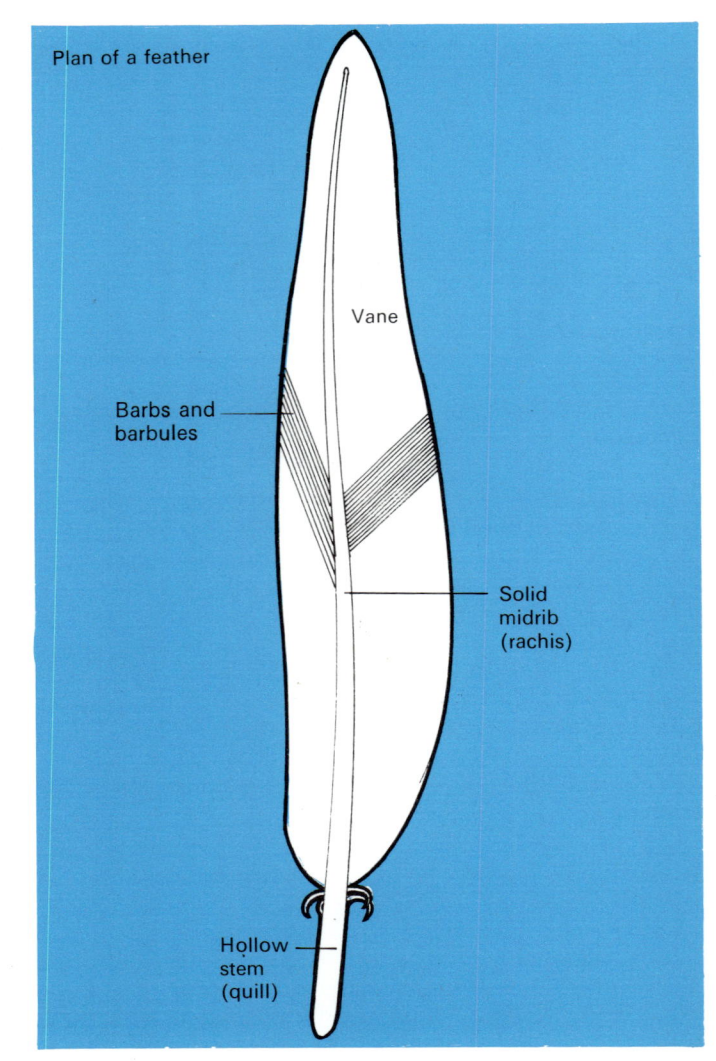

Plan of a feather

- Vane
- Barbs and barbules
- Solid midrib (rachis)
- Hollow stem (quill)

How birds fly

Many children will know from their experiences in the swimming pool that they can propel themselves forward by pushing backwards with their arms against the water. If they think of this when they watch birds flying they will realise through discussion that a bird propels itself forward and upward by pushing backwards and downwards against the air with its wings, that is, they beat against the air.

Stronger pushes are made by continuous surfaces.

Compare the effect of pushing against water with open and closed fingers.

Now examine birds' wings for arrangements that give continuous surfaces for the down beats. Firstly, you may notice the overlapping arrangement of the flight feathers.

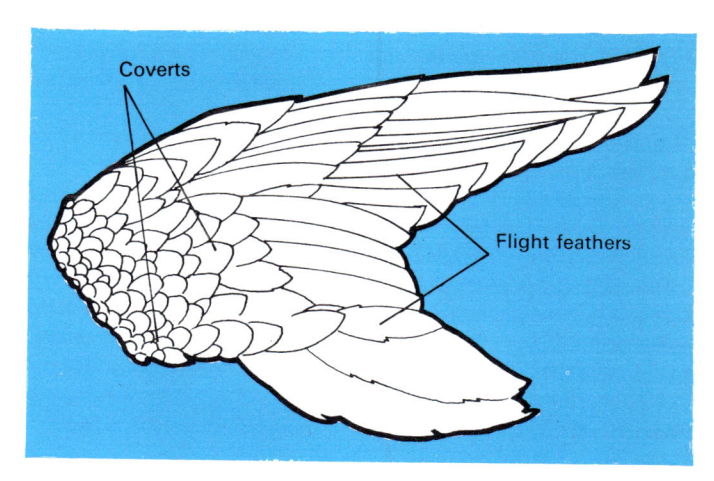

Then with the aid of a stereomagnifier the structure of a flight feather can be studied closely. Stretch part of the vane of a flight feather very gently and observe its continuous surface which is the result of its parts being hooked together. Continue stretching until the parts separate.

During the upward recovery strokes, the wings must be raised quickly so that the bird does not lose height. Certain muscles can alter the position of feathers so that they turn and separate, thus allowing air to pass between them without resistance. Children will not be able to discover this.

The feathers must be kept in good condition. Birds do this by preening, that is rubbing an oily 'waterproofing' material, from a gland situated on the back near the junction with the tail, over the feathers with their beaks. What is the purpose of this waterproofing?

When sea birds are covered with oil slick from tankers they are cleaned with detergent.

Wash a flight feather with detergent. When you have dried it, compare it under a stereomagnifier with a similar untreated feather.

What is the effect of the detergent? Why would it be wrong to release birds immediately after cleansing?

What is done to help them to recover completely from the effects of oil slick?

How does the air help birds to fly?
Watch birds gliding and soaring. Do they seem to be making use of air currents?

Release some fruits and seeds attached to their plumes into the air and try to collect evidence of their movements being affected by air currents. Air has lifting power.

When children of twelve or thirteen have had some experience of air pressure, there are a number of tests they can carry out to compare the effect of differences in air pressure on either side of an object.

An old vacuum cleaner or hair dryer is very useful for creating air streams.

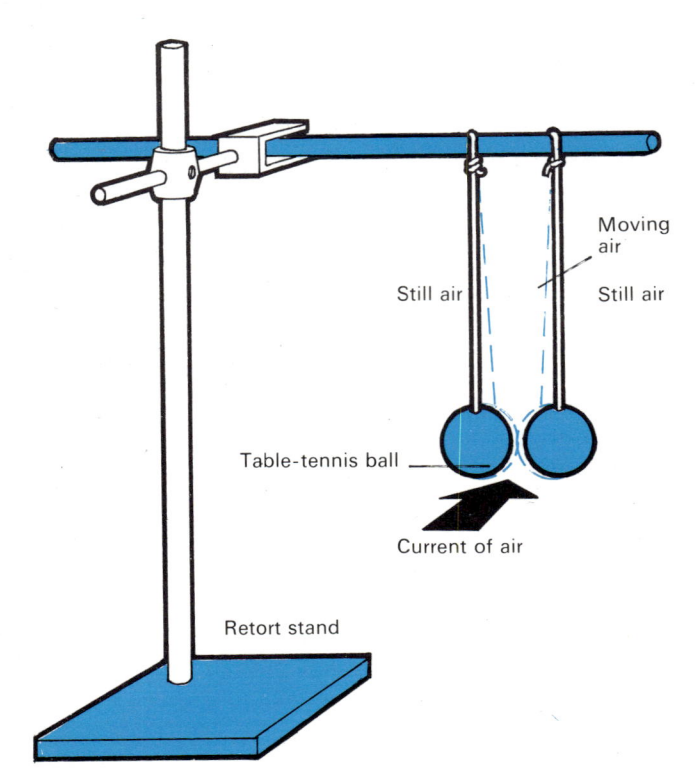

In what way does the position of two similar balls hung as shown change when a stream of air is directed between them? Where was air still and where was it moving when this was done?

Cut a strip of paper 4 cm by 30 cm. Fold over a flap 4 cm in depth at one end. Hold this flap against the chin so that the line of the fold is level with the lower lip, and blow hard.

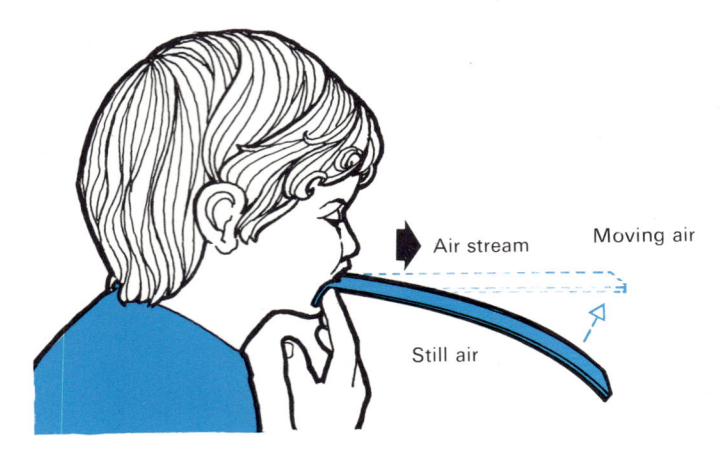

What happens to the long strip of paper?

On which side of it is the air moving and where is it still?

Make a bridge with a strip of cartridge paper. Direct a stream of air beneath it. What happens to the bridge?

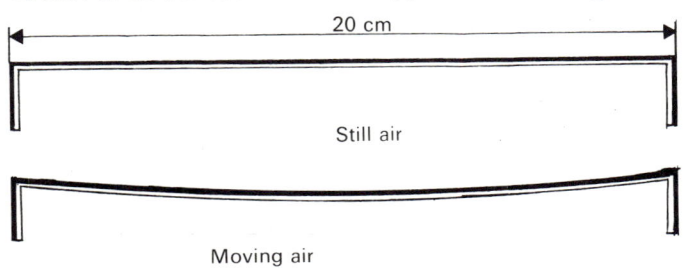

Where is the greatest air pressure in each of these situations, or, in other words, which pushes harder, moving or still air?

Now you can try to work out where air would be pushing hardest on a flying bird.

Compressed air beneath the wings pushes harder than the light pressure of moving air above the wings and this drives the bird upward (ie, gives it lift).

Birds landing

Other movements
Children can try to observe birds performing the following actions:

Balancing.
Turning.
Slowing up.
Landing on the ground.
Landing on water.
Taking off from the ground.
Taking off from water.
Diving.

This could give inspiration for some very interesting creative writing.

The shape of birds

What characteristics give birds smooth outlines when in the air? Does a smooth outline, that is, streamlining, aid movement through surrounding material?

Here is a test.

Obtain some expanded polystyrene balls about 2 cm in diameter.
From a block of expanded polystyrene carve pieces similar in size and mass to the balls but of irregular shapes.
Use a cone-shaped projecting device (obtainable from toy shops or Woolworths) to fire them all: straight upward through the air; forward at different angles.

Which shape travels farthest? Project each shape ten times.

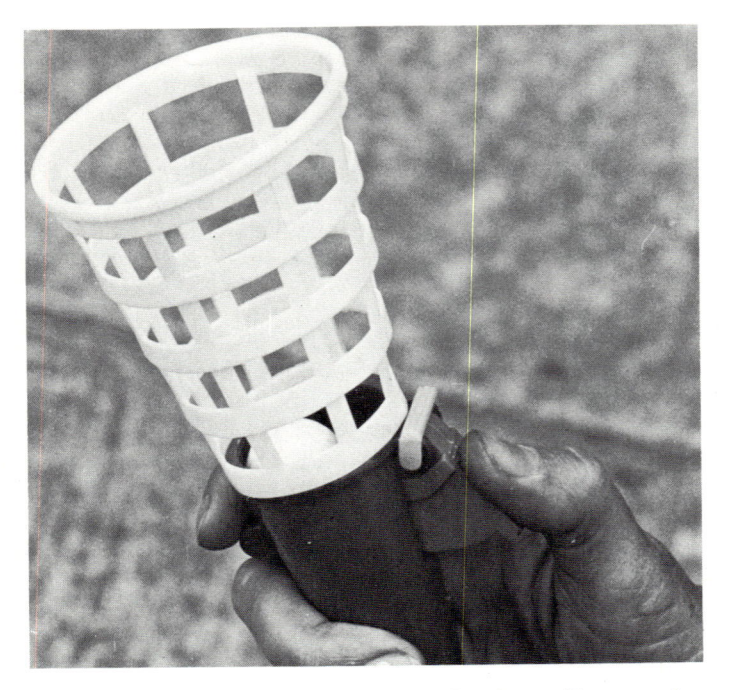

See also Nuffield *O-Level Biology, Students Text* no. 2, pages 69–70 (Longman & Penguin, 1966), for tests on movement of different shapes through water.

Nest building and parental care

What do birds collect for nest building in the spring?

Fill old net tennis ball holders, or the nets in which apples or oranges are sold, with weighed amounts of different nesting materials and hang them on walls or bushes. Make a list of any birds seen carrying material or removing something from a bag. Reweigh each bag after a convenient time to find how much has been removed. Express the amount as a percentage of the original mass.

Make an analysis of any deserted nests found in winter. Weigh them, and then gently pull them apart. Place the different materials for each nest in separate heaps. Weigh each heap. Express each amount as a percentage of the mass of the whole nest.

Results can be recorded on a pie chart.

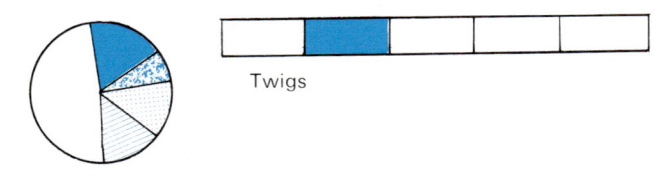

If the birds who used these nests are known, comparisons about the choice of nesting material can be made.

Behaviour

If the school grounds have been designed to attract birds (Volume 4, pages 28–31), interesting observations can often be recorded in spring and early summer about mating behaviour and care of the young.

'One evening hearing a noisy squawking in the garden I hurried to the window. On the bird table crouched a young blackbird while hopping about on the ground below was a similar bird. The mother provided evidence of their relationship for she was trying to feed both offspring. She had a large worm in her beak and in turn tried to push it down each throat. For some time the size and movement of the food defeated her and each time she made another attempt the deprived bird squawked vigorously. At last the bird on the table managed with considerable difficulty to hold and gulp down the offering. Would it manage to digest the meal successfully? The answer was obtained the next morning for at about 8.30 am one bird again occupied the table and the other the ground while their mother searched for worms. At no time was the male in evidence. Did he leave all the work to his mate or was he searching in a different place for food for other members of the family?' (Author's account.)

Making sounds

When children become interested in the sounds made by birds, a collection of gramophone records can prove a most useful aid to recognition. For further details see Volume 4, page 92.

When do birds sing?

Children's reports of sounds heard can be collected on a song chart as their powers of recognition develop, or if their teacher happens to have the type of knowledge and skill that can be helpful.

In this way evidence of the times when birds make sounds or are silent can be built up gradually.

Why do birds make sounds?

Here behaviour could be observed for clues, eg:

Excitement at sighting a supply of food in winter.
To attract a mate.
To warn of danger.
To show aggression.

Which birds select song perches?
Which birds sing as they fly?
When can the dawn chorus be heard?
Which bird makes a drumming sound and for what purpose? (Woodpecker.)
Which bird call is a sign of spring? (Cuckoo.)

If a portable tape recorder is available, children can try to record sounds made by birds when they are out of doors.

Song chart												
Name of singer	Jan	Feb	Mar	April	May	June	July	Aug	Sept	Oct	Nov	Dec
Blackbird					X	X	X					
Thrush					X	X						
Starling												
Common gull	X	X	X	X	X	X	X	X	X	X	X	X
Cuckoo				X	X							

Pieces of cones were used to make this owl

6 Writing about the environment

When children work individually they want to talk and write because they have so many different experiences to exchange. Clear factual reports are particularly suitable for recording scientific activities so their importance may be emphasised in discussion of children's personal records or group projects. It is easier to form good judgements on the results of work when precise explanations of the way it was done are available. Attempts to write these help children to clarify their own understanding while revealing the extent of it to their teachers. Statements must be challenged and arguments developed. However, there will be many other occasions when experiences compel children to say something in prose or verse about the beauty, interest or even tragedy that comes to light as they explore their surroundings.

Personal writing

When the speech and writing of young children comes from a genuine wish to share something it can be very personal. Here are three examples of how children write in their own ways about birds.

The bold robin
A quick flash of wings
That's all you see of timid birds
But the robin
He struts up
And he proudly sings
Waiting for crumbs
That man brings
His breast is a brilliant cherry red
And he's earthy brown
From his head to his tail down
His eyes are like glass beads
As he waits for
The food he needs
That is the bold robin
Olivia, aged ten years.

Still as the snow
Still as the snow lies the dead bird
Its wings frozen
Its blood still
Overcome by cold
The beak open
Its eyes cold
Its body hard
Somewhere in the world lies a nest
And that nest is abandoned.
Michael, aged ten (from the same school).

Christopher (eleven years) never found writing easy, but he liked helping his father look after the chickens. He wrote an account consisting of about 650 words about this, spending a lot of time on it and producing work far beyond his usual standard. Here is a short extract.

Our chickens
When we feed our chickens we give them three feeds daily. One in the morning of mash another feed of mash at dinner but not quite so much as we do in the morning. At night we give them a biscuit tin of wheat. We sometimes get maize (or indian corn). In the wet

weather that is in September, October and November we get maize because wheat would sink into the mud and then we would lose some. But we get wheat to give the bantams, because maize would choke them. In the spring we get maize because it makes the hens go broody and we always want broody hens in the spring otherwise we don't get any chicks. Then we would not have any christmas dinners because people won't have any old cock. They always have young ones, so we get landed with all the old ones. We don't give our chickens corn because corn is wheat, cibled maize, oats and barley. When we give them corn they eat all the maize and oats and leave the rest. Then we waste a lot of it.

Most chickehs like to roost at night in a tree. Our chicken's don't go in the houses at night but they *do* go in the houses when it's raining. They lay their eggs in the houses too, We clean our chicken's houses out about once a week.
Christopher C. S. Broad

It is not only the difference in these children's experience that gives their writing individuality, but also their reasons for giving expression to their thoughts. Olivia wanted to share her own pleasure in a pert garden visitor. Michael sought to arouse compassion, while Christopher was genuinely concerned that anybody keeping chickens should do so properly so he was prepared to give plenty of information supported by reasons.

Many teachers rightly value this personal quality in children's writing for this is what gives it sincerity and vitality, and it is evidence of thought arising from their observations and doings. They wish to encourage it and the best way of doing so is to know and respond to children's needs.

The teacher's influence

Above all children need inspiration. Then they can find something to say. This can only be gained through experience. One of the aims of this book is to draw attention to the rich experience any environment can offer. But the next example shows that the teacher's influence can make this experience more meaningful and so more inspiring to the children.

One day a group of children brought some deserted birds' nests into the classroom and began the usual investigation of materials they contained. Their teacher had the good idea of challenging them to try to make nests. Here is how one child, aged between nine and ten, described what he did.

This afternoon I made a bird's nest. When I tried to weave all the hay in and out I found out how difficult it must be for a small bird. First we made a thick circle of hay and this took ages as we were only allowed to take one piece at a time. I put small pieces of hay in the gaps. Finally I put pieces of hay across the bottom to make a criss cross pattern, then put more clay over them. I smoothed it out but it wasn't as good as a bird would have done it. My nest was very untidy and fell to bits when I tried to pick it up. . . . To be really like birds, we ought to make a nest deep enough to get ourselves into, and strong enough to take our weight. I don't think I could ever manage that . . . I think that anybody who steals a bird's nest ought to have to make another one. They ought to have to fetch everything one piece at a time from the other side of a field and have big cats waiting to catch them if they were slow. . . .

Encouraging children to put themselves in someone else's position can be very effective. In this case first-hand experience brought the bird's problems right home to the writer and enabled him to be most emphatic about the need for conservation. It is a method that can be applied to many other learning situations. Making weapons by chipping flints and drawing and constructing from natural materials, for instance, are good ways of helping children to realise what life might have been like in the Stone and Bronze Ages.

But there can be other kinds of motivation as the next passage clearly shows. The writer found a water beetle while out with the class but was not encouraged to spend time watching the animal after it was safely housed. Instead, she turned to books for this summary of somebody else's experience.

The water beetle
The water beetle is one of the commonest water insects. There are many different kinds. The carnivorous beetle, otherwise called the Dytiscus beetle, is often found in the stagnant ponds where there is plenty of weed. It is

easy to tell the male (♂) from the female (♀) for the ♂ has dark brown smooth wings while in the ♀ they are grooved. They have a second pair of thin wings which they use in flight. They are also good swimmers and excellent fliers. They usually travel from pond to pond at night. If you keep them in an aquarium it is necessary to cover it or they may escape.

The girl who wrote this probably gained her teacher's approval for carefully written, correct work, as indeed it was. She had also learnt a few facts about water beetles. However, these are not really her words, she had no first-hand experience to communicate and therefore the compulsion to share any personal feelings or opinions, so evident in the previous vivid writing about the bird's nest, is missing. Did the second child really wish to say anything about the water beetle to satisfy herself? Or was she motivated by her teacher's wish for a contribution to the class frieze? If the latter, was her time really well spent? Learning to feed the beetle and watching its reactions might have provided better inspiration.

Freedom of expression

When children have something they really wish to say they need freedom of expression. Directions to group their thoughts under stereotyped headings such as 'method', 'result' and 'conclusion' are thoroughly restricting. A request for everybody to write an account at the same time after a shared experience such as a country walk, usually yields little more than the names of places passed and a record of the most conspicuous objects noticed. The following sample is typical of the class output in such circumstances.

When our class went for a nature walk down by the river I saw two pheasants, two black and white sheld ducks. We left our school at 9.15 am and got back at 11.20 am. While we were there we caught shrimps, water boatmen, water fleas and beetles. Christopher caught some shrimps. The river was very rough. Before we got to the bridge we saw the bank. It was sandy soil. When we came back we saw a thrushs nest with eggs which were warm. We saw two swallows. The bank we walked along was cracked because of the sun. There were barges going up the river with paper and wood pulp. On the river bank it was very windy.

A list would have provided as much information as this. It would have been better to encourage the children to select whatever they found most interesting during the outing and say something about that in more detail when they felt ready to do so.

The children in another class tried to rear a fledgling blackbird, Moses, found in a stream. While caring for the little creature they were given no specific directions to 'write about Moses'. However after a time the following entries appeared in some of their diaries, in which they were simply expected to describe whatever seemed significant to them.

'Moses opens his beak wide whenever I lift my hand near him. He does it for a pencil, a stick or a finger.'
'When he is fed the food has to be pushed right into the back of his throat or else he drops it. Perhaps it is because his tongue is hinged differently from ours and it is not easy for birds to swallow.'

'If we had another bird I wonder if it would feed Moses and then teach him to peck for himself?'

'His heart beats very fast and he seems to have to breathe a lot faster than we do. I wonder whether he can stand on one leg when he is sleeping.'

'I wonder how he will know what kind of bird he is. Perhaps it doesn't matter. I suppose birds don't know what they are—they aren't born with names, its only what we call them.'

Here the children's own thoughts as well as their individual observations appear.

Feeding Moses

How differently, too, when they are left free, they choose to describe the scenes and places they observe most closely. Shane (nine years) selected something beautiful and seasonal.

Autumn winds
Down come the leaves
Gold brown and yellow
Whirling, whirling, down they come
Off the oak, apple and pear.
The wind flashes past
The red berries are ripe
And the old man's beard is hanging

Linda (aged eleven) described a far less attractive scene.

The railway station
A smoky dusty smell
Of cigarettes
Burnt tops of matches
Littered discreetly
In every corner
Sweet packets
Old papers
Old tickets
And bags scattered on benches
The night porter yawns
And waves his flag
And blows his whistle.
He heaves a sigh
Then picks up his paper,
His only comfort that dark night.

Finding the right time

In the lines below nine-year-old Ann reveals another need of children who want to write freely and naturally.

It was lovely on the green hill
I sat and thought how beautiful it all was
The green grass and the flowers still.

Children need the right time—time to stare and absorb, time to reflect, and then time and opportunity to write as soon as it seems necessary to do so.

June (ten years) became interested in a crab in the salt-water aquarium. She returned many times to the tank to watch, and little by little her record grew.

I have been watching the crab in the sea water tank. When I feed him I push food down to him on a stick and hold it there while he goes for it with his big hungry claws and strange mouth. Sometimes he takes it off the stick and then it floats away up to the top where he can't reach it.

Some days later:

Today the crab took his food and held it tight in one claw. Then with the other one he picked off bits and fed himself, one-clawed. I think he has learned that this kind of food floats away, because it hasn't got a shell to keep it down like the things he used to eat in the sea. I think we have caught a clever crab.

Later:

I put some tasty bits of fish in an empty winkle shell and he was able to use both claws again. I told my Dad and he said this crab must look like an American when he eats with one claw and I remember seeing them eat like it on TV.

Patricia (ten years) saw a terrified injured hare cross her path during an evening walk. She wrote this poem as soon as she reached school the next morning.

The dead hare
We were walking along the Coney Banks
When all of a sudden it appeared
Its coat red with blood
And it was shaking with fear
We stared at it
It stared back
We stood there
We were stunned
Then it died.

It was better to express at once the compassion felt for a suffering creature rather than store a harrowing memory. The teacher who saw to it that this could happen was a wise person.

Developing an argument

A good way of helping children to include their own thoughts and opinions in what they have to say is through argument. The teacher of a fourth-year junior class who tried this provides the following account.

'We had been interested in the life cycle of the fly and a boy had brought us some gentles from his fishing bait. We studied them in the usual ways and as they went on through their development a child asked "Shall we let them go when they are hatched or shall we kill them?" The children began to argue fiercely about this and it appeared to be an excellent opportunity to attempt debating. Before we could do so a dead house martin was brought to school and again, obvious points of interest were dealt with. As we were about to dispose of the corpse a bluebottle was seen to be interested in the dead bird and we left it undisturbed so that the fly could lay eggs in the bird's open beak. The suggested debate was held up so that this piece of unlooked for evidence in favour of the fly might be taken into account, and when the eggs hatched and the bird began to be consumed from within by the maggots a drastic change of opinion was obvious. This natural cleansing process was a revelation to many of the children especially as it was accompanied by a surprising absence of smell which, to children, is the acid test of cleanliness, and it seemed as if the debate would collapse for lack of opposition to the fly. However, the children decided that there were still plenty of pros and cons, so we held the debate. It was really lively and rewarding as the arguments flew and all manner of compromise suggestions were made:

"Let's kill half and release the other half."
"Let's let them go in the country where they will lay eggs on dead things but won't get on our food."
"That's no good, they'll find people having picnics."
"If it was in Maths you could half kill all of them and it would really come to the same thing as really killing half of them."

'After half an hour the discussion was still lively and ten minutes later we were ready to take a vote. There was a large majority in favour of letting the flies go, largely influenced at the last minute by a girl who had a convincing reminder of some work that had been done on food chains, so they were duly released.

'Next day we were lent a copy of *Scientific American* in which the whole subject of flies and health was dealt with in most technical terms but the children's interest made them ready to listen to extracts and to find out the meanings of several words used in the article. They were also pleased to hear that this latest piece of high level work had resulted in nothing more conclusive for or against the fly than had their own debate—they were pleased that, on this occasion anyway, they had given the creature the benefit of the doubt.'

And so these children enjoyed their argument. The next step forward would be to present in writing the case for and against a controversial matter.

Supporting statements with evidence

Statements must be supported by evidence to be convincing. Long before children become capable of presenting a whole reasoned argument they can develop the habit of backing up the statement they make, as this sentence from six-year-old Paul's writing about the seashore shows.

'The tide has been in and made the sand wet. I know because of the lots of solid sand pies. Dry ones drop down.'

Teachers can help children to develop this more convincing style of writing. When they go through work they can point to a statement and ask 'How did you know that? You might try to tell me next time.' Many children respond to such hints.

Here is how a nine-year-old child used the results of his own work as evidence that rocks should be sorted in a particular way.

I took some rocks (not man made ones) and scratched them with a knife, a fingernail and a piece of glass in that order. The ones that scratched when I used the knife were Marble, Kentish Rag, Sandstone and Slate.

The ones that didn't were the pebble, the Iron Sandstone, Red Flint and the Flint. Then I took *the ones that marked* and scratched it with a fingernail, the ones that marked this time were the Kentish Rag and the Sandstone, the ones that didn't was the Marble and Slate. For the glass marks I took the *ones that didn't mark* when I used the knife and scratched them with the glass, the Red Flint and the Iron Sandstone scratched while the Pebble and Flint didn't mark.

A child two years older who is beginning to think more logically shows (below) through this account of a discovery during a cold spell of weather, that he is well aware that he must look for evidence in order to be certain that his ideas are on the right track.

> One day in February Graham Moore found a dead Shel duck on the marshes near the Nature Reserve.
> It was one of nearly 300 that had mysteriously died. We know that when birds die like this it is nearly always due to the fact that they cannot get a their food supplies.
> It appeared that due to the very cold weather the Estuary mud had frozen solid and the birds could not dig in the mud for their food. After the thaw we went down to the marshes to see if we could find the little mollusc, which is the birds main food. In the picture, you can see us with Mr Hudson searching.
> We did manage to find a few they are called the Laver Spire shell and we have mounted them on the white card. We shall never know for sure whether this caused the birds death but it is the only explanation we can think of so far. The Estuary mud freezing solid is something that has hardly ever happened before in living memory.

He is well on the way to writing as a scientist would do.

Direct experience helping imagination

There will be other occasions when children will wish to turn from writing about things they have done and seen in order to create imaginary stories and pictures, and this is also something well worth encouraging.

In making up this story in which he gives birds human personalities, ten-year-old Michael, the author, has moved away from reality and therefore from a scientific way of writing about the things around him. It is interesting, however, to notice how, when he adds descriptive detail, he still draws on the knowledge of the habits and behaviour of birds which he has gained from his own direct experience of bird-watching. This is a very popular pursuit of many of the children in the village school for their teacher is an enthusiast.

My nature story
Once upon a time there lived a little skylark named Suke.

One day Suke was walking through the grass in the meadow when she saw another skylark and it was a boy skylark. When it saw Suke it went over to her and said 'Would you be my wife' to Suke.

Then another skylark saw Suke so it went over to the other skylark and started to fight it. Soon the first skylark ran away so the second skylark said 'Shall we go and make our nest in a hoof print in the ground?' So they went and found a hoof print and put grass in it. Then Suke went to the farm and got some hen feathers and sheeps fur.

Then a few days later Suke laid four eggs in the nest. When the eggs hatched Suke was delighted. So she and Tim had to get extra food so that they could feed the young birds.

When the birds were older they had to fly. Suke and Tim had to teach them to fly. Soon the babies could fly so they left Suke and Tim.

Then Suke and Tim left the meadow to get some rest from all the hard work they had done.
Michael Chandler, aged ten years nine months.

Ten-year-old Stephen's memories of his own visits to the seashore and his experience of night time helped him to construct this imaginary scene.

The sea at night
No airborne seagull screeches
On the deserted beaches
The sea just laps upon the shore
No children play there any more
The moon just hangs above the sea
Nothing moves except the soft sea breeze
Nothing stirs, nothing wakes
But unexpectedly dawn breaks
At last awakens everyone
And the sea is lighted by the sun

These last two quotations show there is no sharp gulf between writing about reality and imaginative work, though extremes of these styles may vary much more. Whatever they may be trying to do children can only give out something that is already within them. Therefore the teachers who are constantly giving children opportunities of investigating their surroundings and of then, pursuing in school, the many individual and corporate activities that arise naturally from the outdoor experience, are certainly providing them also with the inspiration and means of gaining knowledge from which more than one kind of writing can develop.

These children are getting their inspiration for creative writing from outdoor surroundings

Developing skill and accuracy

The liveliness of much quoted here suggests that many children enjoy communicating through writing. It is essential that teachers should encourage them to do just that. However, the emphasis on pleasure may make some teachers wonder about how they may correct children's work or whether they should do so. There is no doubt that when children really have something to say they should be allowed to do so freely without the distraction of warnings about spelling, tense and punctuation. Their own observations and thoughts put into words are what matter most. Yet there is value in helping children to increase their mastery of their own language through further consideration of what they have written, just as informed constructive criticism helps many adult creative artists.

I had a long talk about this with the headmaster of the school Carole (ten years) attended. She had drawn on her own memories of snow and woodland to write these beautiful lines reminiscent of 'The Listeners' by Walter de la Mare.

A rest in the woods
I was sitting in the woods with my horse,
The man who owns this place is far away in the village,
The snowflakes fall on the ground gently
The wood was growing more beautiful every minute

The journey has been long
And we are both very tired
But my horse must think it strange
To stop in such a lonely place

The flakes curl gently
Guided by the soft moaning wind
Singing bells break through the sound
As my mount shaked his harness bells

I would stay much longer
If I could
But I must be traveling on
But I must be Traveling on

When this is judged by adult standards some note should be taken of mistakes in tense and spelling, but we agreed that children's wishes to say something should not be restricted by a barrage of rules and conventions. It is afterwards, when a batch of work has been completed, that the time may be right for helping children with the techniques of language. There are then two possibilities open to the teacher: class and individual teaching. The teacher may decide to bring agreement in tense more deliberately to the notice of the class through some direct teaching. Thus she can make available to Carole the knowledge she needs either to see for herself what can still be done with her poem or avoid the mistakes in future. Alternatively Carole could be given individual attention. The teacher could let her know of the pleasure her effort had given and then inquire whether the event described happened some time ago or is now taking place. In this way she can indicate that adjustments are needed. Carole could also be encouraged to turn to a dictionary to check the spelling in the last two lines. Some children find individual help most encouraging for it convinces them that their work matters and that their efforts to progress will be appreciated. Only the teacher, knowing Carole, can judge which way of helping will best meet her particular needs.

Another good way of encouraging children to appreciate and be critical of writing is through interest in each other's efforts as well as those of other people. Although it is better for children to concentrate on writing about their own experiences rather than summarising factual information from books, these should be used to help children to notice the different ways in which words and phrases can be used by people in describing their own observations and investigations.

As children move through the upper classes of secondary schools, it may well be appropriate to adopt certain conventions in the recording of scientific work. This will make their style more impersonal. But while they are young and gathering their basic experience, the teacher's aim should be to help them to exploit and share their own observations and opinions by writing in both poetry and prose.

Here are some books that teachers and children might enjoy reading aloud from and discussing.

Prose
Alan Moorehead, *No Room in the Ark,* Chapter 8, 'The Turkana' (Hamish Hamilton, 1959).
Konrad Lorenz, *King Solomon's Ring*, Chapter 11, 'The Perennial Retainers' (Methuen).
Gavin Maxwell, *Ring of Bright Water*, page 33, 'Helping a cygnet' (Pan, 1969).
Thor Heyerdahl, *The Kon-Tiki Expedition* (Allen & Unwin, 1950).
Gilbert White, *The Natural History of Selborne* (Everyman, Dent, 1966).
Charles Darwin, *The Voyage of the Beagle* (Everyman, Dent).
Eileen Soper, *Wanderers of the Field* (Routledge & Kegan Paul, 1959).
James R. Johnson, *The Last Passenger* (Macmillan, New York, 1956).

Poetry
Here are some anthologies containing poetry inspired by the environment. From this material poems relevant to many different situations can be selected.

Poems and Pictures, 'Sea and Shore', 'Creatures Small', 'Colours', 'Weather and Seasons', compiled by D. Saunders (Evans Bros., 1974).
Out of School, compiled by D. Saunders (Evans Bros., 1972).
Mirror Poems by Children Under Twelve, by winners of the *Daily Mirror* competition and others (Ginn and Co., 1970).
L. Clark, *The Year Round* (Rupert Hart-Davis, 1965).
Junior Voices, edited by G. Summerfield, Books 1, 2, 3, and 4 (Penguin, 1970).
Galaxy Books 1, 2, 3 and 4, compiled by J. Forman (Pitman, 1967).

Richard Armour, *Who's in Holes?* (World's Work Limited, 1973).

Objectives for children learning science
Guide lines to keep in mind

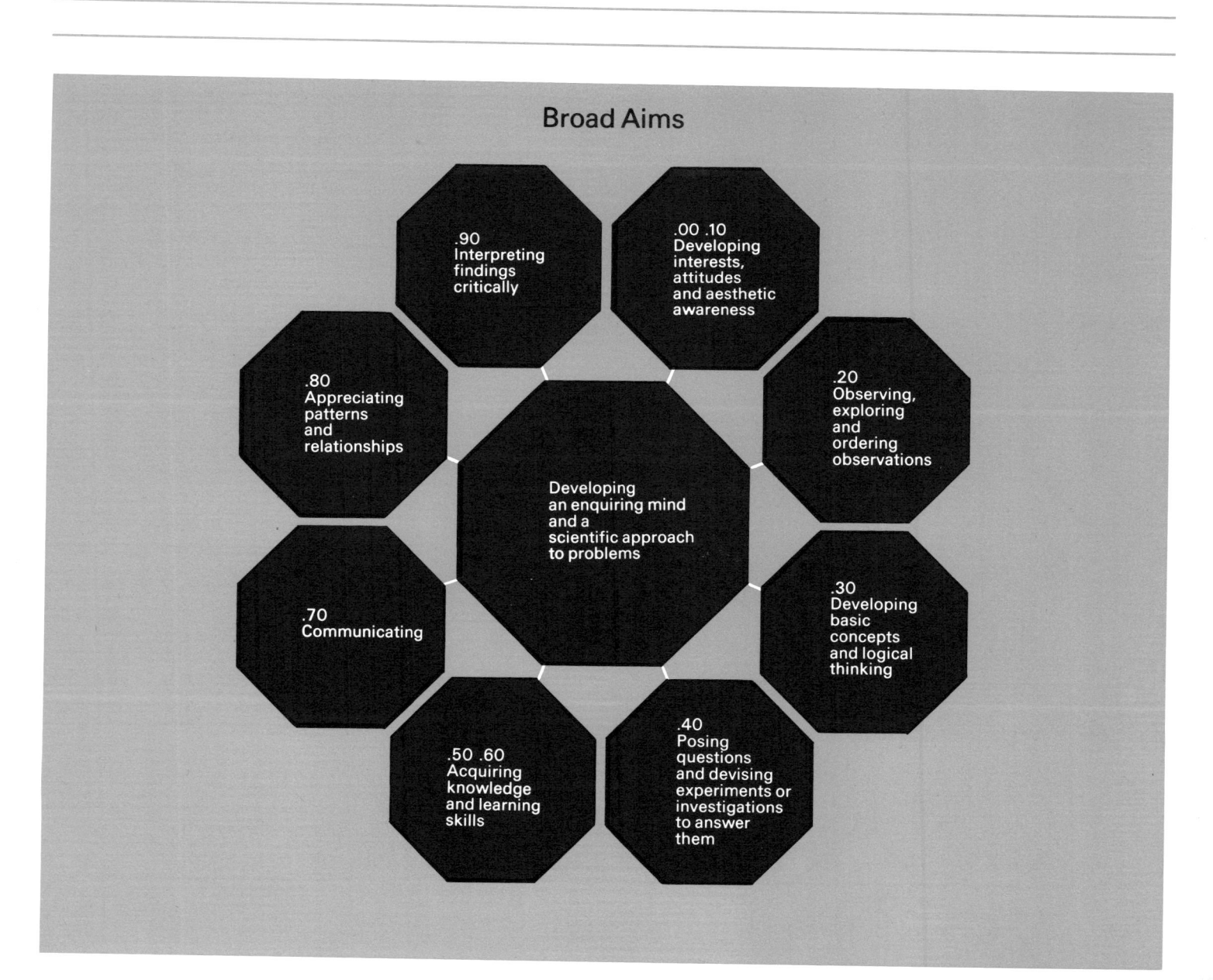

Sc 5/13

Broad Aims

- .00 .10 Developing interests, attitudes and aesthetic awareness
- .20 Observing, exploring and ordering observations
- .30 Developing basic concepts and logical thinking
- .40 Posing questions and devising experiments or investigations to answer them
- .50 .60 Acquiring knowledge and learning skills
- .70 Communicating
- .80 Appreciating patterns and relationships
- .90 Interpreting findings critically

Developing an enquiring mind and a scientific approach to problems

What we mean by Stage 1, Stage 2 and Stage 3

Attitudes, interests and aesthetic awareness

.00/.10

Stage 1
Transition from intuition to concrete operations. Infants generally.

The characteristics of thought among infant children differ in important respects from those of children over the age of about seven years. Infant thought has been described as 'intuitive' by Piaget; it is closely associated with physical action and is dominated by immediate observation. Generally, the infant is not able to think about or imagine the consequences of an action unless he has actually carried it out, nor is he yet likely to draw logical conclusions from his experiences. At this early stage the objectives are those concerned with active exploration of the immediate environment and the development of ability to discuss and communicate effectively: they relate to the kind of activities that are appropriate to these very young children, and which form an introduction to ways of exploring and of ordering observations.

1.01 Willingness to ask questions
1.02 Willingness to handle both living and non-living material.
1.03 Sensitivity to the need for giving proper care to living things.
1.04 Enjoyment in using all the senses for exploring and discriminating.
1.05 Willingness to collect material for observation or investigation.

Concrete operations. Early stage.

In this Stage, children are developing the ability to manipulate things mentally. At first this ability is limited to objects and materials that can be manipulated concretely, and even then only in a restricted way. The objectives here are concerned with developing these mental operations through exploration of concrete objects and materials—that is to say, objects and materials which, as physical things, have meaning for the child. Since older children, and even adults prefer an introduction to new ideas and problems through concrete example and physical exploration, these objectives are suitable for all children, whatever their age, who are being introduced to certain science activities for the first time.

1.06 Desire to find out things for oneself.
1.07 Willing participation in group work.
1.08 Willing compliance with safety regulations in handling tools and equipment.
1.09 Appreciation of the need to learn the meaning of new words and to use them correctly.

Stage 2
Concrete operations. Later stage.

In this Stage, a continuation of what Piaget calls the stage of concrete operations, the mental manipulations are becoming more varied and powerful. The developing ability to handle variables—for example, in dealing with multiple classification—means that problems can be solved in more ordered and quantitative ways than was previously possible. The objectives begin to be more specific to the exploration of the scientific aspects of the environment rather than to general experience, as previously. These objectives are developments of those of Stage 1 and depend on them for a foundation. They are those thought of as being appropriate for all children who have progressed from Stage 1 and not merely for nine- to eleven-year-olds.

2.01 Willingness to co-operate with others in science activities.
2.02 Willingness to observe objectively.
2.03 Appreciation of the reasons for safety regulations.
2.04 Enjoyment in examining ambiguity in the use of words.
2.05 Interest in choosing suitable means of expressing results and observations.
2.06 Willingness to assume responsibility for the proper care of living things.
2.07 Willingness to examine critically the results of their own and others' work.
2.08 Preference for putting ideas to test before accepting or rejecting them.
2.09 Appreciation that approximate methods of comparison may be more appropriate than careful measurements.

Stage 3
Transition to stage of abstract thinking.

This is the Stage in which, for some children, the ability to think about abstractions is developing. When this development is complete their thought is capable of dealing with the possible and hypothetical, and is not tied to the concrete and to the here and now. It may take place between eleven and thirteen for some able children, for some children it may happen later, and for others it may never occur. The objectives of this stage are ones which involve development of ability to use hypothetical reasoning and to separate and combine variables in a systematic way. They are appropriate to those who have achieved most of the Stage 2 objectives and who now show signs of ability to manipulate mentally ideas and propositions.

3.01 Acceptance of responsibility for their own and others' safety in experiments.
3.02 Preference for using words correctly.
3.03 Commitment to the idea of physical cause and effect.
3.04 Recognition of the need to standardise measurements.
3.05 Willingness to examine evidence critically.
3.06 Willingness to consider beforehand the usefulness of the results from a possible experiment.
3.07 Preference for choosing the most appropriate means of expressing results or observations.
3.08 Recognition of the need to acquire new skills.
3.09 Willingness to consider the role of science in everyday life.

Attitudes, interests and aesthetic awareness .00/.10	Observing, exploring and ordering observations .20
	1.21 Appreciation of the variety of living things and materials in the environment.
	1.22 Awareness of changes which take place as time passes.
	1.23 Recognition of common shapes—square, circle, triangle.
	1.24 Recognition of regularity in patterns.
	1.25 Ability to group things consistently according to chosen or given criteria.
1.11 Awareness that there are various ways of testing out ideas and making observations.	1.26 Awareness of the structure and form of living things.
1.12 Interest in comparing and classifying living or non-living things.	1.27 Awareness of change of living things and non-living materials.
1.13 Enjoyment in comparing measurements with estimates.	1.28 Recognition of the action of force
1.14 Awareness that there are various ways of expressing results and observations.	1.29 Ability to group living and non-living things by observable attributes.
1.15 Willingness to wait and to keep records in order to observe change in things.	1.29a Ability to distinguish regularity in events and motion.
1.16 Enjoyment in exploring the variety of living things in the environment.	
1.17 Interest in discussing and comparing the aesthetic qualities of materials.	
2.11 Enjoyment in developing methods for solving problems or testing ideas.	2.21 Awareness of internal structure in living and non-living things.
2.12 Appreciation of the part that aesthetic qualities of materials play in determining their use.	2.22 Ability to construct and use keys for identification.
2.13 Interest in the way discoveries were made in the past.	2.23 Recognition of similar and congruent shapes.
	2.24 Awareness of symmetry in shapes and structures.
	2.25 Ability to classify living things and non-living materials in different ways.
	2.26 Ability to visualise objects from different angles and the shape of cross-sections.
3.11 Appreciation of the main principles in the care of living things.	3.21 Appreciation that classification criteria are arbitrary.
3.12 Willingness to extend methods used in science activities to other fields of experience.	3.22 Ability to distinguish observations which are relevant to the solution of a problem from those which are not.
	3.23 Ability to estimate the order of magnitude of physical quantities.

	Developing basic concepts and logical thinking .30	**Posing questions and devising experiments or investigations to answer them** .40
Stage 1 Transition from intuition to concrete operations. Infants generally.	1.31 Awareness of the meaning of words which describe various types of quantity. 1.32 Appreciation that things which are different may have features in common.	1.41 Ability to find answers to simple problems by investigation. 1.42 Ability to make comparisons in terms of one property or variable.
Concrete operations. Early stage.	1.33 Ability to predict the effect of certain changes through observation of similar changes. 1.34 Formation of the notions of the horizontal and the vertical. 1.35 Development of concepts of conservation of length and substance. 1.36 Awareness of the meaning of speed and of its relation to distance covered.	1.43 Appreciation of the need for measurement. 1.44 Awareness that more than one variable may be involved in a particular change.
Stage 2 Concrete operations. Later stage.	2.31 Appreciation of measurement as division into regular parts and repeated comparison with a unit. 2.32 Appreciation that comparisons can be made indirectly by use of an intermediary. 2.33 Development of concepts of conservation of weight, area and volume. 2.34 Appreciation of weight as a downward force. 2.35 Understanding of the speed, time, distance relation.	2.41 Ability to frame questions likely to be answered through investigations. 2.42 Ability to investigate variables and to discover effective ones. 2.43 Appreciation of the need to control variables and use controls in investigations. 2.44 Ability to choose and use either arbitrary or standard units of measurement as appropriate. 2.45 Ability to select a suitable degree of approximation and work to it. 2.46 Ability to use representational models for investigating problems or relationships.
Stage 3 Transition to stage of abstract thinking.	3.31 Familiarity with relationships involving velocity, distance, time, acceleration. 3.32 Ability to separate, exclude or combine variables in approaching problems. 3.33 Ability to formulate hypotheses not dependent upon direct observation. 3.34 Ability to extend reasoning beyond the actual to the possible. 3.35 Ability to distinguish a logically sound proof from others less sound.	3.41 Attempting to identify the essential steps in approaching a problem scientifically. 3.42 Ability to design experiments with effective controls for testing hypotheses. 3.43 Ability to visualise a hypothetical situation as a useful simplification of actual observations. 3.44 Ability to construct scale models for investigation and to appreciate implications of changing the scale.

Acquiring knowledge and learning skills

.50/.60

1.51 Ability to discriminate between different materials.
1.52 Awareness of the characteristics of living things.
1.53 Awareness of properties which materials can have.
1.54 Ability to use displayed reference material for identifying living and non-living things.

1.55 Familiarity with sources of sound.
1.56 Awareness of sources of heat, light and electricity.
1.57 Knowledge that change can be produced in common substances.
1.58 Appreciation that ability to move or cause movement requires energy.
1.59 Knowledge of differences in properties between and within common groups of materials.

2.51 Knowledge of conditions which promote changes in living things and non-living materials.
2.52 Familiarity with a wide range of forces and of ways in which they can be changed.
2.53 Knowledge of sources and simple properties of common forms of energy.
2.54 Knowledge of the origins of common materials.
2.55 Awareness of some discoveries and inventions by famous scientists.
2.56 Knowledge of ways to investigate and measure properties of living things and non-living materials.
2.57 Awareness of changes in the design of measuring instruments and tools during man's history.
2.58 Skill in devising and constructing simple apparatus.
2.59 Ability to select relevant information from books or other reference material.

3.51 Knowledge that chemical change results from interaction.
3.52 Knowledge that energy can be stored and converted in various ways.
3.53 Awareness of the universal nature of gravity.
3.54 Knowledge of the main constituents and variations in the composition of soil and of the earth.
3.55 Knowledge that properties of matter can be explained by reference to its particulate nature.
3.56 Knowledge of certain properties of heat, light, sound, electrical, mechanical and chemical energy.
3.57 Knowledge of a wide range of living organisms.
3.58 Development of the concept of an internal environment.
3.59 Knowledge of the nature and variations in basic life processes.

Acquiring knowledge and learning skills

.50/.60

1.61 Appreciation of man's use of other living things and their products.
1.62 Awareness that man's way of life has changed through the ages.
1.63 Skill in manipulating tools and materials.
1.64 Development of techniques for handling living things correctly.
1.65 Ability to use books for supplementing ideas or information.

3.61 Appreciation of levels of organisation in living things.
3.62 Appreciation of the significance of the work and ideas of some famous scientists.
3.63 Ability to apply relevant knowledge without help of contextual cues.
3.64 Ability to use scientific equipment and instruments for extending the range of human senses.

	Communicating	**Appreciating patterns and relationships**
	.70	.80
Stage 1 Transition from intuition to concrete operations. Infants generally.	1.71 Ability to use new words appropriately. 1.72 Ability to record events in their sequences. 1.73 Ability to discuss and record impressions of living and non-living things in the environment. 1.74 Ability to use representational symbols for recording information on charts or block graphs.	1.81 Awareness of cause-effect relationships.
Concrete operations. Early stage.	1.75 Ability to tabulate information and use tables. 1.76 Familiarity with names of living things and non-living materials. 1.77 Ability to record impressions by making models, painting or drawing.	1.82 Development of a concept of environment. 1.83 Formation of a broad idea of variation in living things. 1.84 Awareness of seasonal changes in living things. 1.85 Awareness of differences in physical conditions between different parts of the Earth.
Stage 2 Concrete operations. Later stage.	2.71 Ability to use non-representational symbols in plans, charts, etc. 2.72 Ability to interpret observations in terms of trends and rates of change. 2.73 Ability to use histograms and other simple graphical forms for communicating data. 2.74 Ability to construct models as a means of recording observations.	2.81 Awareness of sequences of change in natural phenomena. 2.82 Awareness of structure-function relationship in parts of living things. 2.83 Appreciation of interdependence among living things. 2.84 Awareness of the impact of man's activities on other living things. 2.85 Awareness of the changes in the physical environment brought about by man's activity. 2.86 Appreciation of the relationships of parts and wholes.
Stage 3 Transition to stage of abstract thinking.	3.71 Ability to select the graphical form most appropriate to the information being recorded. 3.72 Ability to use three-dimensional models or graphs for recording results. 3.73 Ability to deduce information from graphs: from gradient, area, intercept. 3.74 Ability to use analogies to explain scientific ideas and theories.	3.81 Recognition that the ratio of volume to surface area is significant. 3.82 Appreciation of the scale of the universe. 3.83 Understanding of the nature and significance of changes in living and non-living things. 3.84 Recognition that energy has many forms and is conserved when it is changed from one form to another. 3.85 Recognition of man's impact on living things—conservation, change, control. 3.86 Appreciation of the social implications of man's changing use of materials, historical and contemporary. 3.87 Appreciation of the social implications of research in science. 3.88 Appreciation of the role of science in the changing pattern of provision for human needs.

Interpreting findings critically

.90

1.91 Awareness that the apparent size, shape and relationships of things depend on the position of the observer.

1.92 Appreciation that properties of materials influence their use.

2.91 Appreciation of adaptation to environment.
2.92 Appreciation of how the form and structure of materials relate to their function and properties.
2.93 Awareness that many factors need to be considered when choosing a material for a particular use.
2.94 Recognition of the role of chance in making measurements and experiments.

3.91 Ability to draw from observations conclusions that are unbiased by preconception.
3.92 Willingness to accept factual evidence despite perceptual contradictions.
3.93 Awareness that the degree of accuracy of measurements has to be taken into account when results are interpreted.
3.94 Awareness that unstated assumptions can affect conclusions drawn from argument or experimental results.
3.95 Appreciation of the need to integrate findings into a simplifying generalisation.
3.96 Willingness to check that conclusions are consistent with further evidence.

These Stages we have chosen conform to modern ideas about children's learning. They conveniently describe for us the mental development of children between the ages of five and thirteen years, but it must be remembered that ALTHOUGH CHILDREN GO THROUGH THESE STAGES IN THE SAME ORDER THEY DO NOT GO THROUGH THEM AT THE SAME RATES.
SOME children achieve the later Stages at an early age.
SOME loiter in the early Stages for quite a time.
SOME never have the mental ability to develop to the later Stages.
ALL appear to be ragged in their movement from one Stage to another.
Our Stages, then, are not tied to chronological age, so in any one class of children there will be, almost certainly, some children at differing Stages of mental development.

Index

Accuracy
  in seed records, 23
  in writing, 109
Air streams, 96
Anemometers, 12
Animals
  adult stage, 32
  books on, 45
  development, 45
  effect on soil, 60
Apparatus, for various purposes, 22
Archaeology, 50, 61

Beans, growth, 28
Beaufort scale, 12
Bird tables, 84, 88
Birds, 82
  distribution, 88
  feeding habits, 90
  flight, 93
  movements, 93
  shape, 98
  skeleton, 56
  sounds, 99
  wings, 94
Books
  on home-made apparatus, 18
  poetry, 110
  prose, 110
  on various animals, 45
Buds, 22, 25
Building materials, 61

Cabbage white butterfly, life cycle, 34
Charts and tables
  animal development, 45
  birds, 85, 88
    flight, 93
    songs, 99
  eggs, 26
  frog tadpoles, 33
  onion growth, 28
  sliding and rolling, 67
Clouds, 8
Compass directions, 15
Compost, 56
Conservation, 33, 62

Corpses, decay, 55
Counting, birds, 84
Cyclones, 58

Daphnia, 41
Decay, 55
Deduction, 106
Digging, 60
Duckweed, 41

Earth moving, 60
Earth worms, action in soil, 56
Eggs, 26
  cabbage white butterfly, 34
Environment, writing on, 101
Erosion, 58
Evaporation, 5
Evidence, to support statements, 106

Feathers, 94
Feeding
  birds, 90
  caterpillars, 36
Food containers, for birds, 91
Fossils, 50
Freezing, 7, 55
Friction, 12, 17, 70
Frog tadpoles, 33, 38
Frost action, 54
Fruits
  collecting, 21
  development, 44

Gardens, preparation, 21
Geological collections, 53
Geological time, 52
Germination, 22
Gradient, 68
Graphs
  birds' feeding habits, 91, 92
  daphnia, 41
  leaf size, 32
Growth, 22, 28, 30

Heating, soil, 54
Hovercraft, model, 72
Hurricanes, 58

Kites, 10

Landscape, 47
Leaves
  measurements on, 32
  seasonal changes, 44
Levers, 75
Life cycles, 33

Magnets, as compasses, 16
Magnification of movement, 77
Maps, 49
Mass, measurement, 30
Measurement
  mass, 30
  rain, 4
  size, 28
  small amounts, 29
Mining, 61
Mirrors, for sky study, 8
Moulting, caterpillars, 36

Nest building, 98

Objectives, 33
Onions, growth, 28

Pendulums, 78
Pie charts, birds' nests, 98
Plants, growth measurement, 29
Playgrounds, 63
  bird records, 88
Population growth, 62
Prehistory, 50
Proportion, 47

Quarrying, 61

Rain gauges, 4
Raindrops, rebound, 5
Rainfall, 6
Records, 4
  birds, 86
  plant spread, 30
  rainfall, 4
  and relationships, 20
  seasonal changes, 53
  seed development, 23

Reflections, 8
Rhizomes, 25
Rocks, 57
   effect of water, 59
Rolling, 67
Roots, upward growth, 25
Rotational movement, 81

Seasons, 53
Seeds
   apparatus, 23
   collecting, 21
   examining, 22
Seesaws, 75
Series, 29
Shadow stick, 15
Shells, 51
Shingle, grading, 54
Size, measuring changes, 28
Sketching
   birds, 83
   landscapes, 47
Slides, 65
Slopes, 65

Snow, 7
Soil, 53, 57
   and animals, 60
   cultivation, 62
   effect of wind and water, 58
   monoliths, 49
Spring, 21
Streams, deposition, 59
Structures, 64
Swan, study of corpse, 56
Swings, 78

Tape recorders
   bird songs, 99
   for observations, 23, 50
Teachers' influence, 23, 33, 47, 102
Telescope, home-made, 83
Temperature, 18
   and bird census, 87
Thermometers, 18
Tombstones, age comparison, 55
Trees
   seasonal changes, 4, 44
   wind effects, 17

Tubular structures, 64
Tunnelling, 61
Twigs, 42

Ventimeters, 14
Visibility, 9
Volume, conservation, 4

Water
   effect on soil, 59
   various states, 7
Weather, 3
Wind, 9
   and bird census, 87
   direction, 14
   effect on rocks and soil, 58
   force measurement, 11
   rose, 17
   sock, 14
   vanes, 17
Woodland litter, 55
Wormery, soil studies, 60
Writing, 101

Illustration acknowledgements

The publishers gratefully acknowledge the help given by the following in supplying photographs on the pages indicated:

Heather Angel, 35 right, 38 right, 39, 40, 51 top right, 72 top right
John H. Cope, 42 right, 43, 44
French Government Tourist Office, 52
Henry Grant, 10, 64 left, 64 bottom right
Eric Hosking, 97
Institute of Geological Sciences, 58, 59
Imitor Limited, 50 left, 50 bottom right, 51 left
Gwyneth Jones, 8 bottom, 30, 104
Kent Messenger, 7 right, 61
Mervyn Rees, 64 top right, 81, 98 right, 100, 103, 108
Royal Meteorological Society, 7 left
Shell Photographic Service, 34 right, 36 left, 37 left
Doris Spicer, 56
Peter Ward, 34 left, 35 left, 36 right, 37 right
Terry Williams, 51 top right
James Wright, 42 left

The following photographs are reproduced by kind permission of W. H. Petty MA, BSc, County Education Officer, Kent, Photographer: M. Williams, 15, 22, 24, 28, 65 left, 71, 82, 89, 98 left

Line drawings by GWA Design Consultants

Cover design by Peter Gauld